TAKE COMMAND!

Vera Dawson Tait

Unity Books
Unity Village, Mo. 64065

Library of Congress Card #80-53217
ISBN: 0-87159-150-2

FIRST EDITION

CONTENTS

Foreword . . . .   *v*

The Debits and Credits of Life   9

Release!   19

Who's Driving?   29

Like Rain   39

All Is Good!—

      Stumbling Block or Truth?   45

God Within   53

We All Need a Bridge   63

Go, Sell, Pay   71

Listen Twice   81

Larger Maps   89

"If I Am This, Why Am I That?"   95

Moments to Remember   105

Your Spiritual Spectacles   113

The Result of an Irritation   123

No Trespassing   135

All Night Coming   145

Destiny at My Command   155

About My Father's Business   165

Foreword

VERA DAWSON TAIT is one of the great teachers in the Unity movement. I am so happy that some of her writings are now in book form. She writes clearly, lucidly, with a depth of understanding of Truth principles, and with insight as to how to apply them. She knows whereof she speaks, for she lives it.

Vera Dawson Tait's enthusiasm for Truth and for the Unity teachings has never flagged. She is a glowing, radiant, joyous example of what it means to practice Truth principles in the everyday issues of life—large and small.

You will find *Take Command!* filled with ideas and inspiration. It will answer many of your questions about the Unity teachings. If you already know Vera, either personally or through her writings, you will rejoice with me in this book. If you are just discovering Vera Dawson Tait, you will come to know and love and appreciate her through the pages of *Take Command!*

—Martha Smock

Take Command!

The Debits
and Credits of Life

IN CONNECTION with financial affairs we talk about "double entry," "debits and credits," "balance sheets," "capital investment," and the like. I like to think that we can consider the business of life also in terms of bookkeeping.

There is infinite justice through all the warp and woof of life. Anything done must somewhere, somehow, be compensated for. In other words, the accounts of my life, of every life, must be kept by "double entry."

God has furnished "capital investment" for me, for every living soul. He has provided ample working capital; He has invested in me all that is necessary to make the business of life a success. What *is* this capital? Where does it come from,

and why does it come? Because God is Divine
Mind, my "capital" must be ideas, love, wisdom, faith, imagination, life, strength, peace,
and all the other good ideas that we can conceive
of. Not only has God given me Himself in the
form of these vital, living ideas, but He has also
given me minute instructions as to how to use
them in the carrying on of my business. The
covenant made by Jehovah as recorded in Jeremiah reads: "This is the covenant . . . I will put
my law within them, and I will write it upon
their hearts." I know now what my capital investment is, and I know it comes from God and
comes because I am His beloved, His son.

With my capital investment and all my direc-
tions for a successful business, I may open my
ledger account. I enter my capital investment,
my consciousness of all the ideas and blessings of
God, on the proper side of my ledger. When I
really stop to consider I am astounded at what I
have to start with; I am surprised, uplifted, encouraged!

I am reminded of a story I once heard of a man
who was bemoaning the fact that he was so very
poor in worldly goods. Suddenly he began to
take stock. He asked himself what price he would

accept for his eyes, and decided he wouldn't accept a million dollars. What would he sell his ears for? Why, not for half a million dollars. His ability to think, to converse, to share ideas, to feel, to be conscious of living—what would he take for these? There was absolutely not wealth enough in all the world to buy these precious assets.

In taking stock of my own life I find that in addition to these precious physical and mental gifts I possess even more precious treasures as I go into the spiritual realm of thought. Of course I am wealthy beyond the wildest dreams of the human mind! My capital is not only unlimited and priceless to start with but, because it comes from God, it is maintained indefinitely without depletion. It is here that I begin to play my part. My capital is not something merely to think about, to lay away unused; it is something that must be put into circulation. I realize that this is one aspect of "expenditures" in my business of life.

On the other side of my ledger of life I am ready to make my entries of what I "pay out," or perhaps I should say "radiate," of that which is mine to use through the Father's love. In every act of my daily life it is my privilege to "pay out" or radiate love, the very valuable investment that brings in such tremendous dividends. My expenditure of love in a situation that is nearly "bankrupt" may be the very turning point for myself or others. Or perhaps this particular condition requires the expenditure of more understanding than I have been using in order to prevent disaster. Perhaps more faith, tolerance, or patience may save an otherwise hopeless situation. Whatever it is, I find that my expenditure brings back to me wonderful returns; it keeps open the channel through which more of God's invested good flows into my life from God, my silent partner.

The business man who knows he has a substantial investment behind him has confidence in every step he takes in his business. By knowing that I have been given much, and that I may call upon divine wisdom and guidance in the handling of my inheritance, I learn to be confident in the use of wisdom in wise decisions at home, in my work, in my social relations. I find my faith much more workable, dependable, firm, because I use it to hold the vision high for someone near me who needs just an extra boost in faith at a particular time. Because I have grasped the truth of who and what I am and what I have at my disposal, I confidently "pay out" more faith in God.

This "accounting" in my life cannot be a mere daydream or theory; it must be a practical, workable thing. I come to realize that the expenditure of the divine idea of health will net me rich returns in my body, so I learn to give the substance of my thoughts not to imperfection and illness but to vibrant, buoyant life. With this new understanding I see that giving out a consciousness of health will teach me to keep the laws of health, for I see the necessity of doing my part in the outer to keep God's temple pure and clean. Through each of the ideas that make up my capital investment I can see what will be the result of proper and wise handling not only in my individual life and world but in the lives of others.

There is another aspect to the expenditure side of life: the debits. When the debits are not legitimate my business of life does not go along smoothly. I must hold firmly to the truth that my credits are always sufficient to take care of every debit. As I give, so do I receive. In order to keep my bookkeeping straight I realize that life is a balance of giving and receiving; that I must do *my* part toward keeping this balance. What can I do then when I get off the track somewhere, when I find myself "in the red"? That which governs my life must be practical; it must not only keep me straight but also serve as the means whereby I can adjust myself when I have not kept the balance.

In business we find that when a man or a company gets "in the red" it means that more has been paid out or expended than there was in the capital stock. There can be many causes for it, such as bad investments. In any event credit has been lost when the debits exceed the credits.

When my life shows more debits than credits: inharmony where there should be peace and harmony, ill health instead of health and perfection, lack instead of plenty and success, I know I have made some bad investments by employing my thought energy at work that is not productive of good, or someway along the line I have disobeyed the instructions for successful living. Somehow I have shut myself off from my Silent Partner and forgotten that I have sufficient capital to meet every situation that confronts me.

I have paid out more than I had in consciousness—that is, more than I was prepared to give—and suddenly I am confronted with a situation that makes me panicky. When fear grips me, I forget "who and what I am"; I see bankruptcy staring me in the face. I continue to give, but in my desperation I am no longer giving good currency but counterfeit: fear, intolerance, suspicion. These are not the coin of the realm to which I really belong, and when they "purchase" imperfections of every kind I am muddled and confused.

In the business world when a man takes bankruptcy his affairs are taken out of his control and placed in the hands of a receiver; so far as possible the assets are salvaged and his debts paid. If it is shown that the business has every chance of recovering its financial health, a loan probably is arranged to tide it over the bad period and give it a fresh start.

When I have "gone in the red" in health, finances, and human relations, when I feel my life to be bankrupt, I too have recourse to a receiver, the divine receiver. "Come to me, all who labor and are heavy laden, and I will give you rest. . . . For my yoke is easy, and my burden is light.'' Joyously I lift up my head and my heart. I find I am not cast off because in my upward march I made mistakes, but the divine receiver takes my life and affairs into His loving hands and gives me the chance to start over again. I relinquish my affairs into His care, not in a resigned or passive way but alert and ready for His further instructions. As I let go of my debts—my fears and anxieties—I begin to make my contact with my capital investment through understanding prayer, meditation, and affirmation of the good I know God has never taken away from me. Through this experience I learn much, especially patience and a deep and abiding trust in God.

Many a businessman has worried himself sick. Some have even taken their own lives because of what seemed a hopeless situation, without even making their plight known to those who might have helped them. God never forces Himself upon me, but He is ready to help me when I make the call. I must *know* with deep inner conviction that He is my receiver in whose loving hands I may place my affairs.

There are many things that can prevent our turning to God for help, and certainly self-condemnation can become a gigantic obstacle in making the about-turn to God. What do we condemn ourselves for? Many times we made mistakes because we did not have full understanding or had neglected to ask God to show us the way; we condemn our failure to keep mind and heart centered upon that which is eternally true while accepting the false impressions outside. Yet much that is worthwhile has had many seeming failures before the final goal was reached. The difference between success and failure lies in whether one gives in to mistakes and failures or learns from them and presses on.

No situation is so great a debit that there is not a divine credit that more than balances it. We have these comforting words from the First Epistle of John: "He who is in you is greater than he who is in the world." When I remember this greatness and *use* it, my life ledger will always balance. I know that happiness is mine only as I give it out from within myself. I know that nothing from without can deplete my store of inner wealth, for this is a kingdom where no one else can enter. I may let my business go stagnant through lack of use and wonder why my life does not yield returns that bring happiness, for it is only as I keep in constant contact with the Giver of life and use His gifts that I keep the good steadily flowing in and through me. To hide my capital, as did the man with the talents, is to prove myself an unfaithful steward not entitled to the increase of good.

The knowledge that life may be handled like a ledger sheet reveals to me my very definite part in the business of life. I know I am not an automaton but a vital partner with God in making real and effective His blessings in my own life as well as in the lives of others. I have to recognize beyond mere intellectual perception the truth that the credits of life always outweigh the debits, and that the debits are not to be feared but are to be seen as glorious opportunities for making God's investment in me a living, active thing. Then no matter what comes up in my life I can ''judge not according to appearance, but judge righteous judgment.'' This means remembering the truth back of the appearance of sickness, lack, inharmony, and then calling into activity the credits of health, plenty, harmony. It is up to me to work with the rules that govern my business of life, bringing success and rich dividends.

Release!

HAVE YOU ever thought that often when the word *release* is used, you automatically think of letting go of something unpleasant? Have you considered how important it is to release something pleasant as well? Does this seem paradoxical to you when all Truth teaching encourages you to lay hold of God's good? In fact, one frequently hears the expression "hold to the Truth."

It is true that all of us do need to release beliefs that are less than good; but it is also true that, when we lay hold of an idea of Truth, we need to release it too!

When an idea comes to mind and we are able to turn it over to God, to the very Spirit of life within us, then it comes alive. After all, when a seed goes into the ground, it must utilize the nutriment of the soil and have the advantage of the wind and rain and sun and—above all things—the light, in order to fulfill its purpose.

Sometimes we will not let go of cherished dreams, so nothing comes of these dreams. Why? Because unconsciously we refuse to release them, we refuse to let them go. Often we hear this idea expressed, "Let go, and let God." Usually when we say this, we think of letting go of something negative, letting go of anxiety or perhaps fear. But we also need to let go of cherished dreams and ambitions if we would see them fulfilled. How do we do this? Accepting the premise that all ideas come from God, we place our dream or ambition in God's care and ask that His will be done. What do we mean by this latter remark?

The moment a person says "God's will," perhaps the thought comes that God's will may be the opposite of what he desires. But we must come to know that God's will is His plan, or His purpose, of absolute good. God's will is that each species of creation shall fulfill itself, according to its own divine image or pattern.

When we get the first glimmer of some possible good (which is, of course, a divine idea seeking expression), we begin to build a mental picture. For instance, if an individual is seeking healing, the thought that he is entitled to such healing, that it is his by divine birthright, may be a revolutionary idea. Once accepted, however, he may tend merely to hold mentally to the idea and not allow it to work in him as healing of his body.

Let us suppose that there is something an individual wishes to do in connection with his work. He could be quite enthusiastic about the idea at the outset, but it may never amount to much because he does no more than surface thinking about it. We need to realize that when an idea comes to us it is a mental seed that needs to be "planted" in our consciousness and watered through our thinking and feeling. In other words, we need to cultivate this seed-idea. If a farmer were to hold on to the seed that he was preparing to plant, and never released it to the soil, what would be the result? There would be no harvest, of course. Sometimes we become conscious of a truth and hold mentally to this idea, but we do not give it a chance to put down its roots, as it were, into the soil of divine substance. Daydreaming is somewhat similar. A person holds on to some good thought, something he would like to have or accomplish, yet he merely dreams about it and allows his mind to go over and over it, but nothing more. He may become very enthusiastic about the idea, but it doesn't produce. Why? It cannot produce because he has not released it and let it go.

Take a simple matter such as a proposed vacation. The individual concerned may think about where he would like to go, but he will not go very far if he spends his time just thinking about it. If he is going by car, he may decide to get a road map that will help him find his way there. If he belongs to a motor club, possibly he will ask for help in ascertaining the best route. If he intends to go by airplane, it is probable that he will contact either one or more airlines, or perhaps discuss his trip with a travel agent. You see, he is doing more than holding on to the idea of a vacation; he is letting the idea go, and with the letting go comes guidance as to procedure.

Early in my study of Truth I discovered that one can become so busy with affirmations concerning healing that he does not give the life-idea an opportunity to express itself through the cells of his body.

When we have an idea, a God-idea, for some desired good, then we must let it go. Our letting go is turning it over to God and asking for His guidance. If the idea has to do with healing, we may do a great deal of meditating on it. We may think about it. We think that if God is life, then that life is given to us because we are His children, heirs to His good. You see how this goes round in the mind? But we need to do more than this if we would really attain the healing we desire. We need to take our prayer to God so that He might fill it with the "spirit." We read that "the spirit gives life." It is only from the Lord, or the indwelling presence of God, that we receive the life which makes ideas come alive and produce.

What cherished ambitions, ideas, or aspirations do you have? Have you allowed them to become enmeshed in negation, anxiety, or fear? For example, the love of a mother for a son may impel her to seek help from a teacher or minister because she does not quite approve of the woman he would like to marry. The wise teacher or counselor does not pray for specific results;

rather, he helps the mother to understand that the real prayer is a prayer for the son's highest good.

Suppose, on the other hand, a mother has seen a woman whom she feels will just suit her son and she comes to a teacher or a minister and says, "Please pray that my son may marry this woman." This is not true prayer either. Her son's highest happiness is really the mother's true desire.

An individual, well trained in a certain line of work, might look toward some particular job and say, "That's the job I want." Is he approaching his goal in the right way? It is very possible that this is not the right job for him at all. If he releases his desire for his right place to God, then he will be guided to it, and it might possibly be the very job he had desired.

Many persons who have been great world figures started out in one particular profession and ended up in another. Winston Churchill was a case in point. He was trained for a military career but he was also trained as a newspaperman. He ended up as a speaker, writer, and statesman.

Have you known someone who longed to return to the place where he was born? If he does so, sometimes there is a sense of disappointment, probably because a picture has been built up in mind and the individual has felt that if only he could return there he would be happy. But it has not always worked out that way, since happiness is a matter of consciousness rather than of place.

I am reminded of one incident in my life when it seemed right to move from one locality to another. I thought I had found the perfect home in the new locality and I was very happy about it. Everything concerning this house seemed to be right. Yet within a few days after having made the decision, it was apparent I was not going to be allowed to have this particular house. The man who had looked at it before I did had taken up his option. I had to work hard with my consciousness to get over my feeling of disappointment at not being able to purchase this house. I realized, though, that I wanted only that which was in divine order, so I let the thought of moving to this new locality go from my mind and decided that commuting would handle the matter. Within a matter of six weeks, however, without any conscious effort on my part, the perfect home was revealed to me in the new locality.

A somewhat similar experience occurred in connection with a winter vacation. I wanted to take my mother to a warmer climate for a few weeks. Figuring up my finances and so forth, I decided that we would go to a certain place. All reservations were made. The night before I was to pick up the reservations from the airline office, a friend happened to come to see us and heard me saying something to my mother about the particular place we were going. She asked, ''Why are you going there?''

I made the remark that this seemed the most reasonable place. This friend said to me, ''My husband and I have a fully furnished home you can have.'' She mentioned the area where I had really wanted to go. She said that we could have their house rent-free. Of course, the result was that I made a change in the reservations. It was a wonderful vacation. My mother and I had friends in this area, whereas we would have known no one in the other location. One of the most satisfying things in connection with this vacation was that I made contact with a friend with whom I had lost track for a number of years.

When we give up, surrender, or release our hopes, dreams, and desires to God, what are we doing? We are allowing the seed-idea back of them to go beyond the mental plane into a higher state of consciousness where it may be filled with God-power and manifest in divine order for all concerned. On the other hand, when we hold fast mentally to the hope, the dream, the desire, it remains only on the mental plane and it is only the "letter." As Paul tells us, "the written code kills, but the Spirit gives life."

Enthusiasm is needed in all areas of our life, but when it prevents our releasing the idea we wish to manifest, it becomes a detriment. Understanding must come first, then we add enthusiasm, but not in an effort to force some good into manifestation. Only as the law of God is allowed free rein in bringing forth the answer to our prayer can we be sure of making the desired demonstration. We learn to take our hopes, dreams, and desires, as the old hymn says, "to the Lord in prayer," and they will be filled with the spirit which alone can give them life or make them manifest. Perhaps this is what the prophet Hosea was referring to when he said, "Take with you words and return to the Lord."

I would like to share with you a prayer I once read, which embodies this idea of release:

Dear Father-God. This day finds me releasing to Thee all my fondest aspirations, my most cherished desires. I no longer seek to insist that my will be done, for Thou hast planned for me the perfect fulfillment of every aspiration. To Thee I commend my heart, my hopes, my all.

Who's Driving?

I'LL NEVER forget being a passenger in a car with some friends. The woman was an excellent "back-seat driver." Finally, in exasperation—almost desperation—her husband exclaimed, "Who's driving?"

There is a parallel here for our own individual life. The question is, "Who, or what, is driving my life?" Are we letting some emotion, some person, some situation, or condition tell us what to do?

If God is the one Creator, then He must be in charge of each individual life, for He is the source of the life, energy, and power that each of us uses in everyday living. However, while God is in charge, we need also to have the realization that He has put *us* in control of our own bodies, environment, and our particular world of affairs.

A car rental company, known in many parts of the world, has as its slogan, "Let us put *you* in the driver's seat." As far as our own life is concerned, God has already put us in the driver's seat.

The Spirit of God has created us and given us instruction as to how to run our lives. To instruct a person in the application of a principle governing some process—driving a car, handling a printing press, a manufacturing machine, or a musical instrument—leaves him free then to go ahead on his own. God has put us in control and has placed within us all that is needed to run our lives successfully.

Sometimes the driver of a car can become so upset by other drivers on the road, either by their lack of courtesy or lack of skill in driving, as to allow his emotions to determine his actions, often with unpleasant results. Impatience, anger, fear, or frustration are emotions that can be disastrous to a driver. They may cause him to lose control of his car; certainly they cloud his judgment in driving.

Often such little things can cause impatience,

frustration, and other unwanted emotions in our life experience—irritations concerning our work, even the things we work with and use in our home—and before we know it these undesirable emotions have caused like conditions that are in turn telling us how to "drive." They determine our actions because we have forgotten that God is in charge of our lives.

We have been given the wisdom to drive our own lives, to step confidently forward into that which is for our highest good. If disappointments crop up or if there are unpleasant things to be met, we can learn to handle them when we know the truth of our relationship to God.

Religionists have been known to scoff at the words of the poem "Invictus" by William E. Henley, thinking that they make man too important.

> *I am the master of my fate;*
> *I am the captain of my soul.*

But because man is important in God's plan, these words reveal a truth of the inheritance delegated to each of us by our loving Father. Our "fate" is our everyday human experience. The "soul" is the mind where we think and feel. God doesn't *make* us think and feel that which is good, but He has instructed us and left us free to act. However, whatever we think and feel will come forth as our "fate," or will be the experience of our lives, for good or ill. Thus are we each to be master of our fate and captain of our soul (master of our thinking and feeling).

In Job we read, "You will decide on a matter, and it will be established for you." Whatever we speak forth (silently or audibly) as the result of our thinking and feeling will be established in our human experience. Herein lies our responsibility for our "fate."

Another verse found in Scripture bears out the truth of this idea of mastery. "For as he thinketh in his heart, so *is* he." As our thinking is joined to feeling (heart), so are we. Thus we can see that each one of us must be captain of our soul, or be in full control of our thinking and feeling if we would bring forth the abundant life of which Jesus spoke.

God created us with the ability to conduct our life in accordance with His divine plan. God is the Architect of this plan, but each of us is, in a sense, a contractor, taking the plan, the material, and the tools to build a life.

Who is in control? Who's driving? We may

allow ourselves to be driven by negative experiences resulting from fears about ourselves, about others, fears about our job, fears about our social relations, fears concerning our finances. Before we fully realize it, these unhappy emotions, with their resultant negative conditions, are driving us, and they may cause us to say and to do things that are not conducive to our good or the welfare of those whose lives touch ours.

As an illustration, let us imagine a fleet of truck drivers starting on the business of the day. It is taken for granted that the trucking company is in charge of this group of trucks and drivers, yet the company expects that each individual truck driver will be in control of his own machine, because his job requires skill in handling a truck. In other words, he will be the one who is driving. To be alert and about the business at hand, the truck driver must know what is going on in the road before and behind him. However, he cannot afford to let his own emotions, his own feelings, prevent his good driving or the right handling of his own truck. He may be aware of those who are not obeying traffic laws or those who are not driving in the highest interest of others. Yet he cannot afford to lose his temper, get upset, frustrated. Otherwise, he will lose the control that belongs to him; he will be allowing other drivers or conditions outside himself to drive. To be alert and ready for any eventuality, he must be doing his own driving.

An article I read once reported on the change that could come to a quiet, perhaps ineffective, individual once he had his hand upon the wheel of a car and realized the power that was his, which if not understood, could cloud his good judgment in driving. It is interesting to consider also another illustration which appeared in the same article, showing how even good emotions must be kept under control.

A young man had just proposed to his girl, been accepted, and had given her an engagement ring. When getting into his car to go home after this experience, the young man was so elated, so exhilarated, that he wasn't in control of his car, though his hands were on the wheel! He wasn't really driving, for his head was in the clouds! With his attention elsewhere, he ran through a red traffic light, causing an accident, though fortunately, not a serious one. All this was the result of emotions of joy, happiness, and love, which had taken over the control of this young man's driving so that he was unable to act in a normal way.

Surely then, what we are seeking in our life is balance, and balance is divine order. This order must apply to even the most seemingly insignificant activities of our life. Many of us have had the experience of trying to do so many things before going to bed that we do not get the proper amount of needed sleep (even though it does vary for different individuals) with the result that we are perhaps too tired in the morning or have not arisen early enough to do the things we had planned. Order needs to prevail in all areas of our life; otherwise we find someone, something, some condition pressuring us to get out of order. When we are in order, we are in control; when we are out of order, something other than the Spirit of God in us is impelling us to unwise actions.

We could say, each one for himself, "Why should I let this emotion, this person, this thing, this situation, or this condition determine how *I* am going to act?" What another person says is his responsibility, but if our reaction to it is belligerent, then we will be responsible for the result—and some result or "fate" there will be!—in our life.

If the critical remark made by another person is correct, then we know the correction must be made without a negative reaction—we determine our own reaction. We cannot afford to react negatively by going down to the same level as the criticizer. Should there be need for some correction in mind, body, or affairs, rather than giving way to pessimism and defeatism, we should go "first to God . . . next to man as God directs" for guidance in making the correction. In other words, we are taking orders from God, not from some negative belief, appearance, or condition, whether it concerns sickness in the body, lack in our financial affairs, or inharmony in our human relations.

We must not attempt to (nor can we in reality) follow the pattern of our neighbor.

The Spirit of God has made me,
and the breath of the Almighty gives me
life.

The Spirit in a man is each man's divine pattern or divine nature. If we truly realize our divine nature we will not find ourselves in bondage to conditions in the outer. With so many things in the world to "drive" us—rising prices, loss of a job or inability to procure one, unwelcome retirement, necessity for change of job or home, illness of self or a loved one, need of finances for education, or the world's problems of famine, fire, floods, earthquakes, wars and rumors of wars—it is little wonder that men and women find themselves being driven by uncontrolled emotions and negative conditions. The uncontrolled or negative emotions must be and can be handled in a positive way when we know who is in charge.

Who or what is driving our life? We can easily discover the answer by the results in our human experience. Have we been upset, anxious, fearful? If the answer is yes, then something other than our own divine nature has been driving us. We have given over the control of our life to something less than our true self.

In Unity's fundamental textbook *Lessons in Truth* these words appear: "No person or thing in the universe, no chain or circumstances, can by any possibility interpose itself between you and all joy—all good. You may think that something stands between you and your heart's desire, and so live with that desire unfulfilled; but it is not true.''

Why can such a statement be given as a truth? Because, as was mentioned earlier, God has not given the control—the driving—of our life to anyone else. We are in the driver's seat!

Like Rain

MAN HAS always had special times of thanksgiving, and history bears this out. Most countries have special times for thanksgiving, though the event will vary much between persons. But true thanksgiving is more than one day set aside to think about and give thanks for our many blessings. Thanksgiving is a vital part of our nature; it is as necessary in our lives as rain is to the thirsty soil.

If your garden is dry and rain comes, there is always refreshment. The seeds in the soil sprout; plants that had wilted from lack of moisture become green and fresh again. "Rain falling upon ready soil" produces two things: growth and increase. Thankfulness, like rain, causes also two important things: first, growth, or expansion, in consciousness, and second, increase in outer good.

What is growth in consciousness? It is getting new, usable, practical ideas; increase in outer good means that these ideas are embodied in the forms that will meet our everyday needs. If a plant were to grow and not produce, it would lose its value; if we grow in consciousness without having a commensurate manifestation, then we have failed somehow. Charles Fillmore says, "Creation is not complete until it becomes manifest in the outer." We need principles, theories, but they must produce, become manifest.

An attitude of thankfulness that does not go beyond a mental and emotional approach and fails to produce has not gone very deep. If I am thankful for the country in which I live, the home where I reside, the place where I work or serve, the friends with whom I associate, then my attitude of thankfulness will make me a better citizen, employee, friend. There will be many practical results, for I will come to know an inner peace and loyalty; I will have the kind of friendships that are fulfilling, and my work will bring me not only satisfaction but the right compensation and interesting associations.

Do you feel that you have nothing to be grateful for in this topsy-turvy world with its wars, its crime, its seeming inequalities? Search your own mind (consciousness) and honestly appraise your life. What have you to be thankful for?

You will recall in the story of Elisha and the widow, Elisha said to her: "Tell me; what have you in the house?" Whenever we read the words *house, room, temple,* or *country* in the Bible, we may interpret these as "consciousness." What have you in your consciousness? Have you gratitude for the many good things in your life, or are the negative conditions and situations clouding that which is good, until you say with the widow in the story that you have "nothing in the house." The woman speaking to Elisha did add these words, "except a jar of oil."

When we look more deeply into our consciousness, we are surprised, very often, to find that we do have something to be thankful for. The result of this thankfulness is to open our consciousness and life to an inflow and overflow of good in whatever form we need at the moment. What has happened? Our gratitude or thankfulness has acted as "rain falling upon ready soil," for the "seeds" of our good are the God-ideas waiting to be made manifest in our life; but like all seeds they must be planted and watered.

I remember a story about the result of thankfulness that impressed me. A family had become very down on its luck, with the father out of work. It became necessary to give up a nice home and desirable way of life to move into a house that to this family was quite undesirable. The husband spent his days job-hunting, and the children were at school, but the wife, despondent and depressed, just sat looking at the four walls of the unattractive house. She hadn't even bothered to open most of the packing cases that contained their lovely as well as practical belongings. One day a neighbor came to call, as neighbors will, to welcome her to the neighborhood, and with her she brought a bowl of beautiful flowers. The woman thanked her and put the bowl of flowers on the bare table in the cluttered room.

After a brief chat the neighbor left, and the woman glanced at the flowers and thought they were too lovely to be on a bare table. Here were the first seeds of appreciation and unconscious thanksgiving. She opened one of the packing boxes and got out a tablecloth. Now the table looked beautiful, but in contrast the rest of the room looked even worse than before. She began opening more boxes. Up went curtains; out came silverware and other family treasures.

By the time the children came home from school, the place was so changed that the little daughter exclaimed, "Oh, Mommy, this looks almost as nice as our other house!" When the husband returned from job-hunting, feeling down and discouraged, he was met with the transformation and his face brightened. The table was set, food was ready, and the whole atmosphere was warm and inviting. You can imagine his feeling of thanksgiving! Of course, the inevitable result of the changed attitude of both wife and husband to one of thanksgiving soon put the family on its feet again, with a job appearing almost miraculously for the husband. Their thankfulness had indeed been like "rain falling upon ready soil" bringing refreshment and productiveness to each one in the family.

For as the rain and the snow come down
from heaven,

and return not thither but water the
    earth,
making it bring forth and sprout,
  giving seed to the sower and bread to
    the eater,
so shall my word be that goes forth from
    my mouth;
  it shall not return to me empty,
but it shall accomplish that which I
    purpose,
  and prosper in the thing for which I
    sent it.

All Is Good!—
Stumbling Block or Truth?

ONE OF the things that often confused me in my early Truth study was the remark made either by Truth teachers or students, "All is good!"

The confusion arose in my mind, because all I had to do was to look around me and see so many things that were wrong. For one thing, I myself had come into the study of Truth because of a need for healing. If all is good, does it follow that sickness is good?

During the period when I was seeking to understand the statement, "All is good," and all that it implied, I came across some remarks by Charles Fillmore that threw great light on the subject, as far as I was concerned:

"Metaphysicians have so thoroughly trained

themselves to say 'All is good' that they gulp down all the unsavory messes of carnality. . . . We differ very radically from those who mesmerize themselves into mental torpor by continually holding the thought 'all is good' and applying it indiscriminately to all that appears.

"Remember that man makes all appearances and names them good or evil according to the pleasure it gives him. God furnishes the raw material, as it were, out of which this appearance is formed, and this is always good, because its pure essence *cannot* be polluted."

Mr. Fillmore goes on to say: "If man combines life, love, substance, and intelligence of Principle in such a way that discord results, let him not lay it to God. Man is a free agent, and in the exercise of his freedom he has left out some factor in forming his world. What this factor is he can only discover by asking God direct and he must not omit to ask with all the fervor of his nature. Depending on some teacher or prophet, present or past, is foolishness and ignorance. 'Ask and you will receive.' "

So much that mankind has found disagreeable and undesirable has been blamed on God by persons who say piously, "It is God's will."

How could God, a God of love, of mercy, of justice, be thought to bring unhappiness and suffering to His children, who are made in His image and after His likeness?

Is it because we cannot bear to take the blame for our own mistakes? Perhaps so, but I prefer to think it is only because we do not know any better.

If we follow the principles of mathematics in working out a problem, we will receive a right answer. Our intelligence tells us that if we combine numbers incorrectly, wrong answers will result. We will have similar results in our lives.

Adherence to the laws of life, which are the laws of God, brings right answers in all areas of our human experience. Failure to comply with these laws can only result in conditions that are far from desirable.

Emmet Fox used an expression, "the mental equivalent" that has come to have much meaning in Truth study.

One person may have an uplifted thought concerning health and his "mental equivalent" of life will be a positive one that will help him to meet and overcome physical inharmony.

Another may have a good grasp of abundance

so that he builds a "mental equivalent" of prosperity, enabling him to succeed at whatever he does.

Another may have a "mental equivalent" of peace and harmony so that his life seems to move along smoothly.

We need to remember also that negative "mental equivalents" produce after their kind.

Yes, it is true that all is good in the realm of the true, the real, but each must ask himself what "mental equivalent" he is holding that will act as a magnet to draw to him what he consciously or unconsciously decrees.

Our "mental equivalents" become the master design around which the circumstances of our lives will be built.

At no time does Unity say that war, crime, poverty, unhappiness, sickness, selfishness, anxiety, fear, disease, and accidents are good. We are always seeking to be free from that which causes us distress and unhappiness.

A musician who plays his instrument in direct contradiction to the rules of harmony may say: "This is all harmony. This is all good." His common sense tells him, though, that discord has resulted through his not applying the principles of music correctly. He knows there is but one solution: to return to the principles. He cannot say of his discords "All is good," yet he knows that all *is* good in the sense that the principles back of music are good.

When you and I face the problems of our lives and the experiences of daily living, we can say in all truth, "All is good," without closing our eyes to what needs changing in our world or in our individual lives.

A friend of mine worked at one time with one of the large pattern houses in New York City. One day I said to her, "When a pattern is brought out is it about as perfect as it can be?"

"Oh yes," she replied. "These patterns are so well prepared that if the user will follow the instructions, the finished article will be exactly according to the original pattern."

I thought, How true this is of our lives! God gave to each of us a pattern for life, which is the Christ within. The instructions are very definite in the form of divine guidance.

In her writings, Florence Scovill Shinn makes this challenging statement: "The imagination has been called 'the scissors of the mind' and it is ever cutting, cutting, cutting, day by day, the pictures man sees there, and sooner or later he meets his own creations in the outer world.''

I have always thought this a fascinating idea. The faculty of the imagination ''cuts'' out of divine substance whatever we have decreed by our thinking and feeling.

What faith perceives, imagination must conceive. However, if the faculty of imagination is not given the right pattern upon which to work, then it can only bring into manifestation something undesirable. Conversely, the right mental pattern or equivalent will bring forth the good we seek.

Of God, we can say, ''All is good.'' Of ourselves, we can say, ''We are working to prepare ourselves to bring forth the good already prepared by God.''

Your work and mine is to know, to learn, and to understand how to apply the laws (ideas) God has already provided.

In one situation we may require the exercise of faith. In another, love may be the predominant need. Another situation may need to have the steadfastness that comes from spiritual strength.

Only by turning to the Father within can we be guided in the use of divine principles (ideas) through the tools of thinking and feeling.

We can say, "Thy kingdom come. Thy will be done in earth, as *it is* in heaven," and really mean it. We come to realize that the goodness of God can be manifested on earth, or in the formed world, if we will take the responsibility that is ours and apply God's laws correctly.

The intelligence within each of us reveals that everything in our world is based on some pattern, good or not good. Over all is the one true pattern of our life, which when followed can cause "pattern-changing" in our imagination or what has been aptly called the "chamber of imagery."

When we say, "All is good," our eyes must be lifted beyond the appearances we see in our outer world. We are affirming that which is true in Spirit or in God's kingdom.

In the book *Lessons in Truth,* H. Emilie Cady gives as one of the denial statements, "There is no evil."

This, as much as the statement, "All is good" has been a stumbling block to many students.

No evil? But there are so many things that are not right in our visible world and in our individual lives! When we say, "There is no evil," we mean that there is no evil in God, in Truth. It stands to reason that if God is the one presence and one power, He could not bring forth that which is less than His own nature—good. When we can realize that sickness in the body is not created by God and is not His will, then we are more readily able to deny from our minds the belief that some condition cannot be changed.

If we have lack in our circumstances, we can say, "This condition is not the Truth, because God did not create it." We are then free to move upward to the realization that God is the source of our good, that God wills only good for us, and that we are inheritors of His good.

All of us have many things to change, and undoubtedly the first thing is our mental attitude. This change must bring us to the realization that God is the one presence, the one power, and then we can say, with understanding of the full implication of the statement, "All is good!"

God Within

IF WE THINK about the things of everyday life, we come to understand what is meant by Spirit, or God, within. Look around you! There is nothing you can see that has not started from something within.

Is not everything you can think of, everything you can see with your physical eyes, the outpicturing of something deeper than the form? Back of every form in the visible world, whether it be houses or furniture or food or clothing or whatever, is an idea.

A home, for instance, represents many things to many people, but we might say that back of the ideal home is peace, harmony, and companionship—all ideas. The ideas take form as the comfort of the home, the beauty expressed in its furnishings, and the companionship of its occupants.

What about the forms that are not good? We find that back of each of these forms is some thought that has been distorted until it has no relation to the original idea that came from the Mind of God. This wrong thought has undoubtedly taken the same amount of mental thought and physical energy to produce the malformation.

In his book *Christian Healing*, Charles Fillmore says, "What a man imagines he can do, that he can do." We were given a wonderful ability, the power of imagination, and if we will use this ability in the right way, we can actually hear God "speaking" to us, not in human words but in communications that the soul can understand.

Imagination is that power or ability which enables us to see clearly that something is possible. It must have been difficult in the days before the telephone was a common household instrument to imagine a voice communicating over great distances through a wire. Yet today this is accepted without question by most people.

Even if we cannot explain the how and why, we need to reach the understanding that it is possible for God to communicate with us. Our faculty of imagination needs to form a mental picture of the presence of God as being within us, not a god far off.

We often hear the remark that God ''gives'' us answers to our prayers, but we need to realize that these answers come to us in the form of ideas. These ideas may flash into our minds in answer to prayer, or they may be conveyed to us through the words of other people, or through books, magazines, or newspapers. God's answers will always fit every need of the moment.

Think of all the ways God has of communicating with you! Think of some of the lovely thoughts that have come to you when you have looked on nature. When we think about the movement of lakes, rivers, and oceans; about the growth of flowers, plants, trees; about the song of birds; about the intelligence that moves through animals as instinct, we cannot help but realize this is God trying to say to us: ''Do you not see My life pulsating throughout My creation? Do you not see I am the one presence and power in your life, even as I am the one life moving in every atom of My creation?''

''The still small voice'' is not a human voice, it is God's communication to you in ways that you can understand. Have there not been times in your life when something so awe-inspiring has occurred that you could not say a word? Yet you felt something deep within your being. This was the ''still small voice'' speaking to you; as Charles Fillmore says: ''the voice that is not a voice, the voice using words that are not words. Yet its language is more definite and certain than that of words and sounds.''

God's presence is reality, but unless it becomes an actuality to our imagination, we put up a barrier between ourselves and God. When we turn in faith to God, our understanding becomes stable and we know His presence within, not merely know about it intellectually because some book or teacher has attested to God's indwelling us. We may not be able to explain it in words, but we know beyond the shadow of doubt that God's Spirit, as our very life, is within us.

A basic Unity teaching is that God indwells us as our life, our breath, as the reality back of every atom of our body. There could be no movement in any nerve, cell, tissue, organ, or bodily function without life—and that life is God. His presence in us as life, substance, and intelligence enables all portions of our body to function in order. If this order has been interfered with, so that imperfection, disease, or sickness appear in the body, then it is necessary to turn to the God presence within, seeking direction as to how the body may be brought back into divine order.

Once I read a book written by two doctors, which impressed me, for it referred to the "wisdom of the body." Instances were cited where the body, unknown to the individual, had produced some remarkable healings. We would call this "wisdom of the body" the intelligence and life of God moving through each cell in divine order.

All of us have had moments when we were conscious of the spirit of peace, the spirit of joy, the spirit of faith, the spirit of enthusiasm, without anything in the outer seeming to give impetus to these emotions.

An enthusiastic person may enter a group of people where the atmosphere is rather dull, and perhaps boring. With his entrance a new spirit seems to pervade. Is this not the Spirit of God moving through him as enthusiasm? Whenever we recognize any of the qualities of good, we may be certain that it is the presence of God being expressed through individuals who have, consciously or unconsciously, opened themselves as channels for God's good to express in the world.

When we are filled with doubt, fear, and sometimes with envy and hatred, there is no opportunity for the God-qualities of life, love, understanding, peace, to come forth. It is when we learn to handle unhappy and uncontrolled emotions that we become clear channels for the expression of the spiritual qualities that are within us, not engendered by anyone or anything in the outer.

We might look at a seed and know instinctively that given the right conditions it will send its roots deep into the soil and later appear as the full-grown plant. Something tells us that this seed grew not from anything in the outer, but from something within itself.

Then we might look into our own life. We see evidence of inner growth. For example, we may have a challenge to meet. Perhaps it is concerned with healing, or with finances, or a problem of human relations. No matter how much we may seek out persons or things in the outer for answers, no matter how much we may seek outer advice, we can never get the true answer to our prayer, except by going to the indwelling Presence. We realize that there is nothing in the outer that is going to bring us the healing we need, the prosperity we desire, the harmony we seek in our human relations, even though all of these may come through outer channels.

If God were not within us, how could we contact Him? In the earth, in the sky, in the water? No, unless He were within, nothing in the without could make this contact for us. People, nature, books, may inspire us to seek God. No one and no thing can "give" us God. Nor does this mean that we are not deeply grateful for all the ways in which we receive our inspiration!

The greatest protection any person can have is the knowledge that God is the one presence within his own being. The true foundation for prosperity is the knowledge that the God-presence within each one of us, even as within the seed, moves to fulfill our needs as we are ready to accept the good. Charles Fillmore made the statement in his book *Prosperity* that "the supply unfolds at the same rate as the need or

ability to use substance is developed.'' This supply is not confined to money or possessions but
covers the needs of all creation, including man.
There are times when we think our greatest need
is for things—houses, clothes, entertainment,
cars, and so forth. Jesus reminded us that if we
would seek first God's kingdom the things
would be ours. On the other hand, there may be
something we are not yet aware of that may be
our greatest need at a particular time. I once had
a gift given to me that seemed quite useless, yet
within a short time this was the one thing I
needed very much. The Father within me was
much wiser than I! Our only safety lies in turning
within to the indwelling presence for light and
guidance in seeking fulfillment of our needs and
the ability to use what comes to us.

As this is being written, I am looking out over
the Atlantic Ocean and in my view are several
seagulls, winging their way across the water and
back over the land. I ask myself: ''How do these
birds know what to do? How do they know
where to go? From whence comes their power to
know and to fly?'' Then I think further: ''There
is only one power. It is the power of God moving

in these seagulls at their particular level of intelligence, bringing the fulfillment of their specific needs."

Jesus said, "You are of more value than many sparrows." Am I not better than a seagull? Do I not have a certain work to do? Are not God's qualities of life, intelligence, and substance important to my life, to the fulfillment of the needs that I may have at any given time? Yes! Within me are the presence and power of God. Within me is the Spirit of God moving to accomplish good in my life. Only my refusal to accept this inner Presence can block its perfect outworking as health, abundance, harmony.

Sometimes we think we know what we want from life, or what we want to do in life. Yet beyond all our reasoning and thought, there is the divine wisdom that knows what our part is in the divine plan and how we are to operate in the outer world. Charles Fillmore touches on man's relation to the divine plan when he says, "Man cannot thwart the divine plan, but by virtue of his own creative or formative power he can turn his part of the work in that plan out of its true course and impede the consummation of it."

Yes, in order to receive guidance concerning

our part in the divine plan we need to turn to God within for the only true fulfillment in our lives.

We All Need a Bridge

"ALL OF US need a bridge." This remark made recently by James Dillet Freeman, the Director of Silent Unity, had quite an impact on me. Mr. Freeman went on to say that no matter what we have to face in life, all of us at times need a bridge over and out of problems, a bridge that will bring us to the place where we have the strength, the understanding, and the power we need to meet the experiences of everyday life.

What would this bridge be?

Surely, prayer is one of the most important bridges that can serve us in every area of life.

Every year thousands of people write or telephone Silent Unity asking for prayer. They may not think of it in this way, but what they are really asking is that Silent Unity act as a bridge by which they may find their way out of some problem. Probably this is the very highest work that Silent Unity can do: to be a bridge of prayer, a bridge of faith.

Silent Unity enables the one who is desperate concerning his own health or the health of another person, the one who is frantic because of lack of finances to meet outer needs, the one who is emotionally upset because of inharmony in his affairs, to bridge these unhappy conditions and come into the assurance that there *is* an answer, there *is* a way out. The one needing help, by writing or telephoning to Silent Unity is saying, "Be a bridge for me that will enable me to step over into that place where I feel I can receive the right answer." That place is, of course, the presence of God. As Silent Unity prays with him, he is strengthened in his own faith that God alone is the source of his good. Through this expansion of faith in himself, he opens all the channels of mind and heart—and perhaps hands—to receive the gift or answer of which he has the most need at that particular time.

There is little doubt that in our human experiences we all have need of bridges. A bridge might be in the form of a relative, a friend, or a prayer group such as Silent Unity. That bridge might be none of these—it might be a book, a lecture, the chance remark of a complete stranger. Whatever it is that leads us Godward becomes an important factor in our soul unfoldment, a bridge to fulfillment.

We need a bridge; we may need many bridges. If we have felt a gulf of separation from everything that is good—which means from God who is the source of our good—then we have to have a bridge that will span this gulf mentally and emotionally.

We have to find our own way to God, it is true; but another can help us, can act as a bridge, can stand with us in our moment of need, desperation, doubt, fear, or anxiety. When one asks another to pray with him, he is saying in effect: "Please take my hand. You know where the bridge is. Will you help me to find it so that I may go across the deep chasm that seems to separate me from God and my good?"

When one person would help another through prayer, what he really does is to take him by the hand, figuratively, and help him to set his feet upon the path that leads to his own divine source, his Father-Mother God.

When a condition of personal illness or that of a loved one seems to weigh so heavily upon us that we feel there is no satisfying answer, we may, by just an impersonal questioning of why man is here and who created him, come into an attitude of mind where we are able to rise above the present unhappy condition. By being able to view the situation from an impersonal stand-point, we are freed from emotional involvement. When we think about God as Creator, Sustainer, the one Presence and one Power, even intellec-tually, we reach the conclusion that there has to be a Creator who continues to be interested in His creation. Would you not say that this new at-titude becomes a bridge to a realization of God as the healing life within us and within our loved one?

Yet it is possible for a person to spend so much time in this meditative mood that he goes no further. Meditation is a bridge in itself that moves us on to that place where we are no longer satisfied just to think about God, no matter how noble our thoughts may be. Therefore, meditation becomes the bridge over which we pass into that more intimate phase which we call prayer. Prayer is far more than merely thinking about God, thinking about the needs of our life or our world. In this phase of mind we talk to God. Like Samuel we say to the Lord of our own being, "Here I am." But we could never be satisfied with just speaking to God; for we long, as we do with a friend, to hear God speak to us. Thus this phase of prayer becomes another bridge which takes us into the inner place of silence where God speaks to us and we listen.

Sometimes a person will ask, "How do you know when God is speaking to you?" God's ways of answering are not always what humanly we desire or expect. Many times what we call a "hunch" or a sudden flash of inspiration is God speaking. However, sometimes His answer is in a very simple or unobtrusive guise. It may be in the words of a friend, or as mentioned, the chance remark of a stranger, a phrase in a newspaper, a book, an article. Who is to say these are not the voice of God, the still small voice? Are not these avenues, which convey the message to us that we need at the time, bridges?

Some of us say that we like to commune with

nature. What do we mean? Does it not mean that we find a oneness with the things that grow, the birds that fly, and the animals that creep or walk? We find an affinity with the sun, the sky, the sea, the mountains, the clouds, yes, even the rain, the wind, and snow. Perhaps we cannot explain why we have this feeling. Yet this feeling goes much deeper than it appears to us humanly. This feeling touches a chord within us.

Who is to say that this communing with nature is not a bridge that brings us into the presence of God, or the "secret place of the Most High," as the Psalmist calls it? We hear His voice—not as a human voice—but as a message that is saying: "All is well. I am in charge of My world. I am in charge of your life."

Even our disturbed feelings, because of headlines in our daily papers or news on television or radio of strikes, wars, catastrophes, can, if we turn instantly to God, be a bridge to assurance of God's presence in His world. God is at work in the elements or in the conditions that men produce for themselves. We can make our desire to alleviate undesirable conditions truly a bridge. Thus we can become a powerful center of peace, understanding, love, and good judgment in our individual world and in the world at large.

If we were to look in a positive way into our past, we would perhaps be astonished to find the number of things or people who have served as bridges. Perhaps we have not been fully appreciative of these bridges along the way.

As I look analytically back into my own life, I realize that many people have acted as bridges for me. At the time I may not have thought of them as such. I may have even thought of some of them as causing me unhappiness. Look into your own life and you will surely see where other human beings have acted as bridges, because they have impelled you to seek God. As mentioned, there may have seemed a deep chasm between you and the good you longed for, yet somebody came along just at the right time and proved to be a bridge that made it possible for you to move from a place of helplessness to a place of fulfillment.

You have read or heard the statement: There are many channels but only one Source. We are grateful, of course, to God the Source, but let us be grateful also for the many channels that act as bridges enabling us to reach that plateau of assurance where we have a deep knowing that

God is in charge of our life and all is well.

Yes, we all need a bridge at times. And when we need a bridge, it is there!

Go, Sell, Pay

LOOKING BACK NOW, after years of studying and teaching Truth, it seems strange that there is one important point that I never quite grasped. In fact, it is something I never even thought of. However, after rereading a book I had read and taught a number of times—*Soul Power* by Ernest C. Wilson (now out of print)—I came across a statement that hit me like a blinding light, whereas I had missed this particular point in the past:

"What we do after a prayer has been answered, a need supplied, a dream fulfilled, impresses me as being at least as important as what we do in our time of need, before the answer comes."

The author then goes on to refer to the Biblical story of Elisha, the widow, and the cruse of oil, and he brings out a vital point:

"Through steps of progression from a problem to its solution . . . we come to the admonition, 'Go, sell the oil, and pay your debts.' "

In short, something has to be done *after* the solution to a prayer—for Elisha gave definite instructions: "Go . . . sell . . . pay."

The author says further, "This is a point in 'demonstration' that is often ignored." The more I thought of this, the more certain I became that he is right. I could see that I had ignored it, never having recognized the principle involved. Following this latter quotation is the challenging question:

"Do we allow ourselves to think: 'Well, now that's over! I can relax!'? . . . What we attain in a certain way must be sustained on the same level of equivalence."

The book gives a number of illustrations, such as that of the man who prays for or desires a job but does not sustain his ability or his talent; the businessman who raises the prices of his product without improving its quality (or having legitimate reasons, such as rising costs, for doing so);

the workman who does less than his best, for many reasons. In fact, all who let down their standards have failed to sustain what they had attained. The section of the book from which these quotations are taken closes with words that cause the reader to think deeply on this subject:

"No healing, no blessing is complete until we have 'paid our debt' to God, to ourselves, and to others."

This new vista of Truth has become a real challenge to me. Perhaps you have longed with all your heart for the answer to some prayer, or fulfillment of a need, and suddenly—either in a quiet, normal way or in a rather dramatic way— it has come. What have you done *after* the first thrill of the demonstration? It is taken for granted that you probably gave thanks silently or audibly. However, were you guilty of saying, perhaps unconsciously: "Well, now that's over! I can relax!"? As I look back, I think that in some cases I must have unconsciously gone beyond an attitude that would allow me to relax, for often I *was* able to sustain what I had attained, through faithfulness to prayer and spiritual study. Having this point brought home to me in a more striking way has caused much soul-searching—and it will do as much for you too.

Let us say you have a need for healing, and you desire it with all your heart. You feel that the healing of the condition is about the most important thing that could occur. Faithfully you follow instructions for the changing of your negative mental attitudes, and seek to do in the outer whatever you are guided to do. You do the affirmative mental work that is necessary to open your mind (conscious thinking and subconscious feeling) to the healing power of God. You think of your relationship to God, the source of your life. Having accepted the proposition that you *are* an heir of God, you begin to accept the logic of the Truth teaching that the life which produces health in the physical body is your birthright. You faithfully watch your thoughts to keep them centered on God as the very source of your life. If doubts or anxieties creep in, you firmly take control, perhaps telling yourself that in spite of appearances to the contrary, healing *is* being made manifest. Then comes the time when you suddenly realize that the condition that caused so much distress is either showing improvement or healed. Your whole being responds in praise and thanksgiving. But (and be very honest) are you now in danger of saying, in essence: "Well, now that's over! I can relax!"?

Let us say you have a need for a more tangible form of God substance—money. You turn to God in prayer, realizing that He is the source of your good. Then you begin your faithful prayer work to educate your consciousness to accept the Truth that in reality there is no lack, that whatever you have a legitimate need for is yours in divine order. Once more you had done your work—and I use the word *work* advisedly, because it is both mental and physical work to hold fast to the Truth that God is the source of your supply. "God is my help in every need." You make this a part of your consciousness, your thinking and feeling. You hold firmly to this thought, in whatever words appeal or seem right to you. You give thanks to God that He is opening up the avenues through which your tangible good may come. Then—as in the case of healing—the supply comes to take care of the need, or you are given guidance to handle the need in other ways. Whatever the answer, you *know* that "the prayer has been answered, a need supplied, a dream fulfilled." What do you do then? Do you say: "Well, now that's over! I can relax!"?

Let us imagine that there is a situation of in-harmony between yourself and a loved one, or between yourself and a friend or co-worker, which is causing distress to you (and undoubt-edly to the other person involved). You are con-vinced that only God's love can bring about har-mony. Once more you begin your mental and spiritual work to put your own consciousness in tune with God's laws. Faithfully you hold to the Truth that God is the love and harmony working between you and the other individual. You pray, audibly or silently, using affirmations that seem to fit your specific case. Then, as with the demonstrations in both healing and prosperity, the inharmonious condition is dispelled as a shadow before the sun. Your heart is lifted in praise and thanksgiving to God that peace and harmony are established once more in your human relations. But how long do you hold to this attitude of elation? Are you in danger of thinking: "Well, now that's over! I can relax!"?

It is good for us to give some thought to situa-tions such as these, and to consider what we have done *after* conditions from which we sought relief have changed for the better. We need to ask ourselves if we have "settled down" when a problem has been settled satisfactorily, of if we have gone ahead into life's experiences with more certainty about the Truth so that we were able to sustain what we had attained.

You may recall that Elisha told the widow to borrow vessels from her neighbors, and when these were filled, no more were available. But *after* the supply came (the filling of the vessels with oil, which is comparable to the filling of our consciousness with the Truth), Elisha follows with very practical instructions for outer acts: the widow was to go forth, sell the oil (translating it into whatever was the medium of exchange), and then pay the debts against her and her sons. Metaphysically, we cannot "settle down" after the visible answer to a need or desire, but definite action is indicated which requires the "payment" to God of our love, our gratitude; "payment" to ourselves by translating the ideas back of the answered prayer into whatever we have need of—more steadfastness, more inner assurance of our true relationship to God; "payment" to others in the form of more confidence, more love and compassion, and above all, a deeper realization that they too, as children of God, are seeking to express His goodness in spite of any appearances to the contrary.

The answer to our prayer, or need, has actually put us on a higher level of soul unfoldment, but we need to sustain what we have attained. We are further along the path of spiritual unfoldment through the demonstration, small as it may seem. We can move from this point to a new conception of ourselves, others, our world, and above all, of God.

What will we do *after* "the prayer has been answered, a need supplied, a dream fulfilled"? It depends on whether we are really conscious of having grown in Truth and not merely of having "made a demonstration" of some outer, material thing or changed condition. The demonstration (as we often term the successful working out of a spiritual principle) can so point the way to spiritual mastery that we need less and less to "demonstrate," in the sense of having to handle a problem. Our demonstration then becomes exactly what the word really means—"a showing forth" of spiritual laws, rather than merely overcoming an outer problem.

When Elisha told the widow to go the second time, it had to be an "act of faith." This command deals first with changes necessary in our own consciousness before it is possible for the answer to come. So it is still a further act of faith to "sell the oil, and pay your debts." Rather than settling down into the happier situation brought about by the answer to our prayer, we take this as a signal to go into the new and higher state of mind which guarantees that we will be able to meet successfully the circumstances of everyday living.

Too often those who have been studying Truth a long time, in terms of human years, can become somewhat smug concerning answered prayer, unless there is a great deal of vigilance. All of us need to understand that Truth is ever new, and none of us can rest today on yesterday's demonstrations. Instead of "settling down," we work with the Truth we learned yesterday. The constant fresh approach to Truth study, and adventurous application of the principles and the techniques, enable us to sustain what we have attained.

Listen Twice

HAVE YOU had the experience, as I have had, of reading something or hearing a speaker make a remark that suddenly clicked in your mind and you wondered why you had never thought of this particular idea?

Some years ago I read a short article, not even a full page, that contained a message that has stayed with me through the years. I kept the article tucked away in a book and ever so often would glance over it.

This article was recalled to mind recently when I came across these words in the Bible, "Once God has spoken; twice have I heard this; that power *belongs* to God." It was the word *twice* that made me think of the article, which began with these words of the Greek philosopher Zeno, "The reason why we have two ears and only one mouth is that we may listen the more and talk the less." The article went on to say, "How strange it is that when we talk to God, we often do not do any listening at all! We pray very earnestly and sincerely, but when we have finished, we go on about our business or else begin again to worry about our problem. . . . Take time for a moment of prayer . . . then take two more moments to listen for your very special guidance from God." "Once God has spoken; twice have I heard this; that power *belongs* to God." The thought that came to me was that God "speaks" but once, in that His revelation is given for our acceptance. The first time you and I hear, it is with the intellect, or as Zeno puts it, "We have two ears." This gives us much food for thought, for we realize that our second hearing must be with the more interior hearing, or the inner ear of the soul.

In dealing with anything in our outer world we "hear" first intellectually, with our surface mind. We see this every day in the most simple occurrences of our life. Something takes place that does not impress us very much, perhaps.

This would be "hearing once." But if the event has something of value to offer us or is sufficiently important that it goes deeper than our consciousness, we give it more consideration and we "listen twice."

If we hear only that which appeals to the intellect, we have only the shell, as it were. Were we reading a book, watching a play, listening to an opera, and had we responded only with our minds and not with our hearts, we would have only the "letter," completely missing the "spirit" in any of these events.

Let us consider this idea in connection with our soul growth. If we go no further than thinking about God or even talking to God, never allowing Him to speak to us in the silence, we have listened once and will have only a superficial understanding, or the "letter," of His divine laws.

"We have two ears and only one mouth . . . that we may listen the more and talk the less." If we think about these words, we will have to admit quite honestly that there have been many times when we have talked and talked to God but have given Him little opportunity to speak to us, to reveal His truths in all phases of our life.

We have undoubtedly recounted our problems, those relating to our own individual life and those concerning other persons. We leave the impression that until we tell God what we are facing, He is unaware of our needs.

Too often we have not been willing to wait on the Lord by entering that inner sanctuary of the silence where God does the speaking and we do the listening. It is only in the second listening that we will ever learn what the solutions are for our problems, for any unhappy condition of our life.

Jesus, in speaking of the necessary things of everyday life, said, "Your heavenly Father knows that you need them all." The second listening assures us that God not only knows what we need but is supplying the fulfillment of those needs.

Have you ever had the experience of being so engrossed in some task that you really did not hear what was being said to you because, as we often say, you gave only half an ear? A recent comic strip brought this home to me. The husband was reading a newspaper when the wife said something. He merely gave a kind of grunt, which indicated to her that he had not heard a word she had said. To test him out, she said something very outrageous and once more he replied with no comprehension by saying, "Yes, dear." This, of course, is laughable, but it ceases to be a laughing matter when we are so absorbed in our own problems that we fail to hear what God is saying to us.

The dictionary states that the root meaning of the word *problem* is "to throw forward" and that it is "a question raised . . . for solution." Only God has the solution to our problems, but how can He give us answers if we have listened only once, when we have not given Him our entire attention? We need the second listening period. The answer may be no more than a sense of well-being, a realization that all is well. There may come the unmistakable realization of God saying within us, "I am in charge."

Unless the second listening has become a habit, one has really only heard God intellectually, thus relegating Him to second place in the God-man relationship. The vital mission for each of us is to be sure that God is given first place.

Sometimes when an individual is reminded that the intellect alone cannot save him or give him his answers, he is inclined to downgrade the intellect and think it has no place. But the intellect connects us with the ideas of God that relate to spiritual things and make us aware of the world in which we live and of other human beings who are on the same path of unfoldment. The intellect, or thinking faculty, must be recognized for what it is—a channel or vehicle, but not the Source. Charles Fillmore said something pertinent in this regard:

"Intellectual understanding comes first in the soul's development, then a deeper understanding of principle follows, until the whole man ripens into wisdom."

It is this deeper understanding of principle that constitutes the second listening.

"Once God has spoken; twice have I heard this; that power *belongs* to God." All of us are grateful for people and things in our world that act as conductors for God's good, but "power *belongs* to God." Others may tell us about the power of God, but we need more than this. We need to hear God speak to us of His unfailing power to right all situations and conditions.

As you read, as you study, as you take time for daily meditation, be sure that you "listen the

more and talk the less" to the loving Father.
Then you will have "twice . . . heard"—first
intellectually and second, spiritually.

Larger Maps

IN HIS BOOK *Know Thyself,* Richard Lynch writes: "A British prime minister, addressing Parliament once said, 'Gentlemen, we must study larger maps.' "

A friend visiting in New York City, met a man who invited him to his home. The thing that most impressed the visitor as he was shown over the house was that at the foot of the bed of each of the man's three children was a map of the world. The father explained that the maps were there so that upon awakening each child would see the map of the world and realize that he was a part of a much larger society than just the immediate family circle.

Like the children in the story, we all need to

see ourselves as part of a larger world and also to know that we have a vital part to play in this extended world. We need to have "larger maps."

These words by James Dillet Freeman challenge all of us: "Standing on the shore of an inlet, you may see only a small and agitated stretch of water. You cannot guess at the deeps, the wonders, the boundless extent, the meaning of the sea. Absorbed in the little deeds of every day, the commonplace duties, the momentary needs, you may not see the true meaning of life."

Surely, this inability to look into the deeps of life has caused millions of human beings to see no further than the "commonplace duties, the momentary needs." Most of us need help in enlarging our vision.

To quote further from *Know Thyself:* "Our vision is limited by our proximity to this or that phase of life, which prevents a true interpretation of life's full meaning. Until we are able to enlarge that vision so that we may see, not merely what is obvious and superficial, but the vast magnificence of the totality of the whole, we shall miss the great things that a more extended vision would reveal to us."

While it is true that you and I do need to study larger maps in order to understand our world and our fellowman, it is vital that we discover and study larger maps for our individual self.

One thing of which Silent Unity has long been aware is that there are people who feel they are not needed, not important. Always in such cases Silent Unity has sought, through its letters and literature, and especially through its prayers, to help such individuals get a "larger map" of themselves so that they might come to know their real worth and true place in God's world.

It has been said that "the most important psychological discovery of this century is the discovery of the 'self-image'. Whether we realize it or not, each of us carries about with us a mental blueprint or picture of ourselves." We are told in the Bible that we are created in the image and after the likeness of God. This vital point of Truth must become an integral part of the self-image that emerges as each of us enlarges the map of our personal awareness.

Having had a friend who was in the map-making business for years, I have come to see that there is an art to reading a map. When we have found our "map" we will undoubtedly need help in its interpretation. If you were contemplating a trip to a place where you had never been before and you needed a map to help you, it would be logical to go to the place that, or to the person whom, you felt could supply such a map. If you belonged to a motor club, you would probably go there, requesting an outline of the best route for your proposed trip.

It is true that in our spiritual life we need maps, and certainly the Bible can give us these. However, as in our secular life we need help with a map, we need help with an interpretation of the mental and spiritual maps. Books, courses, lectures, teachers, ministers, all help us to interpret the maps of our life, thus enabling us to enlarge the present map (self-image) of ourselves. But far beyond these outer helps is the revelation, inspiration, and guidance that we receive from God in answer to our earnest prayers. As we turn within to our loving Father for His help, it is always forthcoming. Our prayer may be no more than a simple statement of Truth acknowledging His presence in our life as the guiding light. Perhaps some statement in a book or by a teacher has caused us to pause and think of the meaning back of the words. By turning to God in prayer, we open our minds and hearts to His revelation, inspiration, and guidance. Herein lies the value of prayer.

Many of us have built a concept of ourselves that is far from the true picture of us as sons and daughters of God. We have judged only by the appearance and circumstances in our human experience. If we are not happy within ourselves, we are not going to find happiness outside ourselves. This does not imply that we are to remain satisfied with what we are presently experiencing in mind, body, and affairs. Rather, the maps we are endeavoring to follow should be revealing who and what we are, based on the Bible, upon what we learn from the life and teachings of Jesus Christ, and from all that touches our life for good—whether through close family association, friends, books, education, or society in general. As we seek through prayer and study to enlarge our present maps, we will be able to move along the path of life more easily.

Are new ideas stretching your mind? Are you studying and following larger maps that lead to broader horizons in life?

As the movement of life takes us upward, we

will find still larger maps unfolding as we are ready to take steps that lead us higher. "A mind stretched by a new idea, never returns to its former dimensions."

"If I Am This, Why Am I That?"

IT HAS BEEN a question in my mind whether or not other seekers after Truth had the same question that I had: "If I am this spiritual being that teachers, ministers, and students of Truth assert that I am—this being created by God in His image, heir to all good—why am I in my everyday life that creature seemingly subject to limitations of every kind in mind, body, and affairs?"

Even now, with years of study and teaching behind me, I find myself, when faced with some limitation, asking this on occasion. When I become aware of my "downward thinking," I correct myself with a satisfying answer that brings uplift and comfort. Yet if I find myself meeting this question time and time again, I know that others viewing their life must meet it also.

The Bible tells us in definite terms that "God created man in his image, in the image of God created he him; male and female he created them." Then we may turn to Psalms and read in the eighth chapter a question that my own heart has asked through the years, "What is man that thou art mindful of him, and the son of man that thou dost care for him?" (And somehow my own mind wants to add to this question, "in spite of his shortcomings and ignorance?") Then comes the reply that surely must be inspired by the very Spirit of God: "Yet thou hast made him little less than God, and dost crown him with glory and honor."

If man, then, is this being "little less than God," why the sickness, the poverty, the wars—all the limitations that belie the statement that he is crowned with "glory and honor"?

In the early days of my study in Truth I felt this to be but mockery and mere "word play," but through the years I have come to realize that if I *am* this being created by God, I am *always* this in my essential nature, just as in its essential nature the pansy seed remains potentially the perfect pansy, even if it is planted in such poor soil that the plant proceeding from the seed is weak and its flowers inferior. Then why am I that person suffering sickness, financial problems, loneliness, fear, frustration, anxiety? There must be an explanation somehow tied up with my original creation . . . and there is!

If I am the image-likeness of God, included in my creation is the freedom to act on my own. Charles Fillmore puts it this way: "This is individual consciousness, freedom to act without dictation of any kind."

Note the word *dictation*. This does not preclude God's guidance, for Charles Fillmore goes on to say: "God does not dictate man's acts, though He may instruct and draw him through love away from error. Without absolute freedom of will, man would be an automaton."

With this enlightenment I am coming to the place where I can bridge the "this" and the "that." It begins to make sense to me that though I am *essentially* this exalted being, "a little less than God," I am in the process of bringing this forth into my daily life. Like the student at school, I am learning lessons that bring me closer to releasing what Browning

terms "the imprisoned splendor"—the "this"
of my own being. Thus my real study of Truth
(not just a surface reading of words that make an
appeal) shows me just where I stand in the whole
creative process.

Dr. Ernest C. Wilson seems to have made as
his theme of preaching and teaching words that
become at least a partial answer to the question
under consideration: "Transiently (that is, in
terms of consciousness) we are sons of earth; but
eternally, in the true nature of being, we are sons
of God and heaven."

In another place Dr. Wilson states, "Al-
though we are eternally sons of God and heaven,
we have submitted ourselves to the discipline of
experience, learning by trial and error, which are
characteristic of this plane of manifestation."

Considering these statements of individual
freedom, I am only the "that" in a transient
sense, showing the limitations and "unripeness"
of an evolving son of earth. No matter what
limitations I may be manifesting in my human
experience, I remain always "this being"—
radiant, unconquerable, victorious, free!

How I am expressing the truth of my real self
is influenced by many factors in the transient

phase of my nature: (a) my stage of soul unfoldment; (b) the environment in which I find myself; (c) what I have done—or not done—emotionally, educationally, and physically to handle life's experiences.

There are times when I can say, to paraphrase the words of Jesus, "Father, forgive me, for I knew not what I was doing." Nevertheless, once I have awakened to the truth of my being—that I *am* essentially "this being" above circumstances and environment—it is incumbent upon me to begin bringing about changes in that transient phase, with its shortcomings produced mostly by ignorance, sometimes by willfulness. The good changes allow that phase to become a clear avenue of expression for God's image-likeness.

To accept the belief that I am no more than an unhappy, sick, poor individual with no expectation of change would be like a dressmaker or a tailor seeing many flaws in a garment in the making, yet not being farsighted enough to see that a return to the original pattern would not only indicate the imperfections but would reveal the method of change. Dressmakers and tailors, even the best of them, have to make changes when a garment does not fit the person or the pattern. The Bible presents our divine pattern clearly. Coming to know ourselves as the persons we really are indicates the changes necessary in our thinking, our speaking, our actions.

No one need remain ignorant of the nature of his original creation, but reconciling the difference between the "this" and the "that" is not so simple. It requires not only deep intellectual study but willingness to accept much in the beginning on faith. It requires moment-by-moment vigilance in thought, word, and deed to cleanse and rebuild the "that" to make it worthy of the "inner splendor" that seeks to be made manifest.

If we stop to think seriously, it is a cause for surprise to see that we human beings can find reasons for mistakes in outer conduct, yet refuse to see that there are also reasons why "I am that limited creature" when Truth reveals that "I am this good creation of God."

If the pianist strikes a discord, almost automatically we think, "He did not abide by the rules governing music," or "He is ignorant or careless of the laws of harmony." What about the discords of life that cause us to cry, often in anguish, "If I am this, why am I *that*?"

Most of us do not admit (as glibly as in the case of the musical discords) that "I did not abide by the rules or laws of God governing my life," or "I was ignorant of God's laws of harmony, so inharmony or discord has come as a result." Instead we too often seek an *outside* cause for the consequences we find intolerable. We would look askance at the piano player who sought a cause outside himself as excuse for poorly produced music, would we not?

If you are this spiritual being, with the capability to control the experiences of your own life by the God-power indwelling you, then you are only transiently a limited and frustrated being. Once the knowledge of your divine self becomes an inner knowing, you are well on your way to handling the gulf between the "this" and the "that." You no longer look outside yourself for answers. You know that only as your eye is kept single to God can you ever hope to bridge the chasm that seems to separate you from all that is good and desirable. You know then that prayer is your true lifeline.

Jeremiah tells us in unmistakable terms that the rules of life are written in man's inner being: "I will put my law within them, and I will write it upon their hearts.'' The law is the method or manner in which a principle is expressed. We may be sure that God has already provided a built-in set of instructions on how to apply the principles of life. It is true that we may need outer help from teachers and books to recognize the laws and learn their right application. We must accept the truth that these laws of life are indeed within, inscribed on our own minds and hearts. It should not be difficult for any of us to accept the fact, as well as the truth, that each cell of our physical bodies has its own pattern and mode of functioning.

If discord or disease does occur, it stands to reason that outer remedies may in some cases be required, until such time as the obstruction to the free expression of life in any organ or function can be removed. When the free flow of un-obstructed life takes place, we, often in awe, term it a "miracle."

No doubt the body really seeks to express the purpose for which it was created—to be about the Father's business of providing a vehicle through which its true nature may express.

The golfer learns to keep his eye on the ball; the painter and the sculptor must keep their vision centered on the object being reproduced on canvas or marble; the musician must be true to the composition he seeks to interpret. Once convinced that I *am* this being created by a loving Father, in His own image and after His likeness, I too must be centered in the Truth I would interpret and reproduce. Through prayer, through discipline in thinking and feeling, I learn to erase from my mind and life experiences all that is less than the divine pattern of myself.

Moments to Remember

RECENTLY A FRIEND let me read a delightful little book written by a retired schoolteacher in the Kansas City area who had taken a never-to-be-forgotten trip around the world. Because she wanted to retain, as she says in her book, "instant remembrance of events," she kept extensive notes. On her return home, the notes and pictures were put together and combined in a little travel book under the title "Moments to Remember."

When I read the book I was very much impressed by the author's insistence on retaining moments of that round-the-world journey so that she might relive it in memory. The thing that struck me was not so much that I was reading a travel book, but that one individual was focusing on good events to retain in memory.

Suddenly I became aware that all of us have "moments to remember" in our *spiritual* unfoldment. Yet how often we are more inclined to hold in remembrance the difficult, the unhappy, the undesirable! What would happen if, in the midst of some negative problem that is demanding our entire attention, we stopped to focus our minds on some of the lovely moments—the moments of victory, the moments of overcoming—for these are more worthy of remembrance. What are some of these "moments to remember"? Would they not be such as a time we were able to overcome some physical disturbance; the sudden flash of light or inspiration that came in a perplexing situation; the gratitude we felt at the healing of a loved one or friend for whom we had been praying; the supply that came in what seemed like miraculous ways to fulfill a need? These are indeed our "moments to remember."

Probably most religions seek to instill in their followers the need for gratitude, for thanksgiving. It is true that we often find it difficult to arouse a sense of thanksgiving when facing a trying situation. I am reminded of an illustration that appeared in a Unity article: if you were walking along a beach by the sea or beside a lake or a river, and you reached down to pick up a pebble and lifted it to your eye, this small pebble would almost blot out the entire landscape before you.

Too often some problem, like a pebble before our physical vision, obscures the landscape of our life, of our world, and of the people of our world.

Suppose you *do* have a health challenge to meet. Your attitude toward it can be like the pebble held to your eye, or it can be a stepping-stone to higher ground.

One of the advantages of daily study and prayer is that these influence our thoughts in the right direction. But thought alone cannot do it; we must move beyond the intellectual into the feeling that health is ours by divine right. Thinking, coupled with feeling, removes the pebble of fear and anxiety, so that the mind opens itself easily to the inflow of guidance and healing. Perhaps it is possible to think of other moments of healing that have taken place. These "moments to remember" may be the very lever that will help you to rise above the health problem you are currently facing. It is amazing how much *feeling* can be engendered just in remembering victories of the past.

It is true, we are continually urged to live in the present. That which is good cannot remain in the past but becomes a vital part of the present. We need to look squarely at the Truth that provides the motive power for overcoming. In the case of a condition of ill-health, we must accept the Truth (and feeling is required for acceptance) that our God is a God of life and that this life has been bequeathed to us for our use and enjoyment.

If you feel you have fallen short of adherence to the laws of health, then you need to know that you will be guided to do what is right to provide the conditions for this God-life to express in every area of your body temple.

If the Holy Spirit is "the whole Spirit of God in action," according to Charles Fillmore, then we need to build this truth into consciousness. Like a "bank deposit," it can become for us a "moment to remember," to be drawn upon at a critical time when the mind and body have need of this assurance.

Suddenly you are faced with a lack of money

to meet some financial obligation; panic grips your mind and acts like the pebble before the eye, for it blots out the Truth that there *is* supply to meet your every need. Somehow statements and platitudes seem to leave you cold. But a mental recall of a moment when you had faced the same type of situation and came out victoriously lifts your whole consciousness, and you can say to yourself, "God *is* my supply, and I know that He is taking care of everything." It is like dropping the pebble that was held before the eye, for your whole viewpoint is changed into a larger approach to the situation. Where before there was only panic and confusion, now comes assurance and peace. You turn your attention Godward; you say in essence: "Father, humanly I don't know what to do in this situation, but I do know that supply is already provided. I trust Thee to guide me in handling this problem." Sometimes rather than many words, I find myself praying, "Father, I know Thou art in charge of my life." Then comes the type of peace that clears the mind for the next step.

Even in handling problems in human relations you will find the method to be essentially the same. The misunderstanding, the quarrel, the bitterness, like pebbles before the eyes, need to be removed by remembering moments when God's love smoothed out situations that seemed insolvable by human methods. The problems of the shaky marriage, the unsteady business, the alcoholic bondage may be viewed in the light of those other moments: the love that led to the marriage, the thrill of starting the business, and the strength and freedom of the one who is seemingly bound to an unhealthy habit. The "moments to remember" may constitute the first step in the climb out of the negative ruts in which individuals find themselves.

But our "moments to remember" are not merely related to the overcoming of negative experiences! They have become part of our "book of life." We remember the stories of Jesus, His teachings, the incidents in His life, and we are thrilled all over again. The old hymn states: "Tell me the stories of Jesus . . . And I shall fancy His blessing resting on me." The secret lies in the word *feel*. This is what our "moments to remember" do for us—arouse feeling. The author of the book, to which reference was made at the beginning of this article, says in the preface: " . . . like taking the trip all over again.'' I can attest to this, for while visiting the incomparable Alhambra at Granada, Spain, a few years ago, I recorded my ''moments to remember'' by tape in a cassette recorder. I find that in listening to what was recorded, it is indeed ''like taking the trip all over again.'' So it is with our ''moments to remember'' in Truth—they *spark* feeling in the present moments when we have great need to know that the same God-Truth that proved itself in actual living in past experiences is just as able to meet the challenges of today.

Our ''moments to remember'' are enabling us to feel God's blessing in our lives today. Herein lies the value of books or periodicals of daily inspiration, such as *Daily Word*. We may be inspired at the moment of reading, but the greatest value lies in the inspired action that follows in daily living, handling the business, dealing with other human beings, meeting the hourly challenges of human experience. What may have thrilled me in the morning and given me courage to meet the day's experiences may also cause me to make the right decision in some vitally important matter involving others. Many a businessman has found that some simple remark read or heard in a morning meditation or study period has been the very anchor to which he has had to hold in the stress of some business transaction. Then he is able to file away, as it were, the knowledge of what has been accomplished in some situation that can become one of his "moments to remember" when meeting a similar experience in the future.

There are so many lovely things in life that are like jewels, bringing added beauty and joy—the love and companionship of loved ones and friends; the experiencing of moments in quiet, secluded places or in the pulsating life of great cities. The appreciation of God's world adds many "moments to remember" in the adventure we call "life."

Your Spiritual Spectacles

EARLY IN my study of Truth through the Unity presentation, I began to wonder about the help one received from ministers, teachers, and books of inspiration. I found that I was continually being advised to seek the Truth from within myself, yet when I read Paul's words in Romans 10:14: "But how are men to call upon him in whom they have not believed? And how are they to believe in him of whom they have never heard? And how are they to hear without a preacher?" I knew I was in agreement. I thought of the word *preacher* as meaning *teacher* and realized that without the help of the friend who had first introduced me to what we term "Truth" and the subsequent books and teachers, I would have been no further ahead, for these outer means showed me how to seek within.

It was at this point I realized that in a sense ministers, teachers, and books were as "spectacles" to my mind. Of course, I knew that spectacles were eyeglasses; and because I like to delve into meanings, I checked the dictionary and found that spectacles are "a pair of lenses fitted in frames and worn in front of the eyes to aid the vision." This had real meaning for me and I found that this has followed me through the years. It was of particular value to me when I became director of the now-discontinued Unity Correspondence Course, and it is still of value in teaching. In the third chapter of the book *Lessons in Truth,* which was used in the Correspondence Course and is still used as Unity's basic textbook for study, these words appear: "My advice is: If you want to make rapid growth toward spiritual understanding stop reading many books."

It was not really surprising to me that a number of students, on reaching this place in their study, questioned the above words. Some even went so far as to drop the correspondence work. Having been faced with this same problem in my own study I could understand, sympathetically, what they were facing. However, it became necessary to explain to the students that they had taken the words literally without seeking an explanation. The words in *Lessons in Truth* are really to prevent students from becoming confused through outer seeking in many books. In searching for guidance, very often it is wise to stay with one book, concentrating on the ideas under consideration. However, many can attest to the guidance that came in their early days of study as they read first this book and then another. But this did not lead to confusion, rather a point made in one book often amplified a former statement from another source.

As I mentioned, I could thoroughly understand a new Truth-seeker's concern at the suggestion that he stop reading books and seek within himself, having been through it myself. I know how grateful I was to teachers and books, especially in my early study. I was so mentally hungry to know more that I read as many books as I could, like a starving man reaching out for physical food. I did not get confused, as I felt that my heart was unconsciously asking God for guidance in learning that which would lead to unfoldment. There came a time when I discovered that I could read an entire book and get out of it only *one idea* that was needful at that stage. Then as I went along in my study, I realized that one page gave me much food for thought; then came the time when a paragraph became an entire lesson. As the years progressed, I found that often a single sentence could give me a whole new world of thought.

If eyeglasses are a temporary assistance to correct a defect of vision, to make clear that which we desire to see in the outer with our physical eyes, or in many cases an aid until such time as the eyes can see without this help, then we come to realize that this is true of our "spiritual spectacles" also.

In the ninth chapter of the book *Lessons in Truth* are some words worth considering in this regard: "Books and lectures are good, teachers are good but you must learn for yourself that Christ, the Son of God, lives in you; that He within you is your light and life and all. When you have once grasped this beyond a doubt with the intellect, you cease looking to teachers to bring you spiritual insight. . . . Teachers talk about the light, but the light itself must flash into the darkness before you can see the light."

The important statement here is, "cease looking to teachers to bring you spiritual insight." This does not mean that teachers (and books) bring us nothing. They, being of the outer, often give us the impetus to seek the inspiration needed, but they cannot bring spiritual insight. It does not mean that you will no longer enjoy books, teachers, ministers, discussions of Truth with friends—rather, you will have a much greater appreciation of them—but it does mean that you will be looking deeper for the truth, or spiritual insight. When a statement in a book or a remark from some speaker finds a responsive chord in your heart, you will feel that you have found a new friend! It becomes a confirmation of what has been revealed within.

You will recall that when Jesus asked, "But who do you say that I am?" Simon Peter replied, "You are the Christ, the Son of the living God," and Jesus answered him, "Blessed are you, Simon Bar-Jonah! For flesh and blood has not revealed this to you, but my Father who is in heaven." Not even Jesus could actually reveal the truth concerning the Christ. I have always had the feeling that there must have been a sense of wonder even in Jesus that the answer could have come to Peter so directly from the Father within him.

The study of Truth may seem at times somewhat paradoxical in that on the one hand we advise the use of spiritual spectacles through books and teachers, then on the other hand we suggest ceasing to rely or depend upon them. If we see our spiritual spectacles primarily as aids, instruction guides, to the deep place within ourselves where the presence of God may be consciously found (not that it is ever lost), then we are putting our spiritual spectacles in their right place.

There is always a danger of leaning too much on outer aids, in any line of endeavor. The danger is that they loom so large in a person's consciousness that there is a temptation to see them as a source rather than a channel. The musician who leans only on the techniques has no feeling in his music; the writer who concerns himself only with the spinning of words and phrases loses their inner meaning.

Scripture makes very clear the point that light comes only from within: "God has revealed to us through the Spirit. For the Spirit searches everything, even the depths of God. For what person knows a man's thoughts except the spirit of the man which is in him?'' So, at best, any teacher, preacher, or book can only present ideas of Truth; they bring us to the door which we ourselves must enter in order to learn of Spirit that "searches everything, even the depths of God.''

Sometimes a person may close his eyes to the good to be found in ways other than those which he has felt were right for him. He then loses help that could put him steps ahead in his soul unfoldment. This is especially true if there is too much leaning upon an outer teacher. If that teacher should be removed for any reason, then the student feels bereft and refuses to seek further. This has occurred time and time again. We need to be very grateful if one set of spiritual spectacles has served us well in finding our way of Truth. However, we must be willing to lay them aside, if circumstances cause a severing of the association, and be ready for a new pair of spiritual spectacles.

No matter how wonderfully a person may write a book, an article, preach a sermon, or teach a class, these are but channels for the presentation of ideas. Unless these ideas become food to the individual soul, they will remain in the intellect as the "letter" and not "the spirit [that] giveth life."

There is a native intelligence throughout all life as part of our built-in equipment as human beings. However, the child cannot read a book until he has learned his ABC's, nor can he play a musical instrument until he has learned the notes and rules of music. Most things we have to learn intellectually, and this is true of our spiritual study. If anything seems easy it is probably because in our soul's evolution we have already learned that very thing. Those who have helped us to learn have earned our gratitude. This sense of gratitude should reach out to those who have been our spiritual spectacles. There is a tendency sometimes on the part of Truth students to be so grateful for the opening up of spiritual truths that they fail to be grateful for the church or organization that brought them thus far.

Everything in the outer—ministers, teachers, books, organizations—that has taken us by the hand and led us into a new understanding of life needs our deep-felt "Thank you." We should be thankful also for books of inspiration to be picked up and read occasionally, or for devotional aids such as *Daily Word* that become our help at the beginning of our day and seek to lead us to that deeper place where the Spirit reveals the truth to us.

Have you ever picked up eyeglasses belonging to someone else and tried to see through them? You probably laughed and said, ''I can't see a thing!'' This is just as true of our spiritual search. We cannot see by another's spiritual spectacles, and if we try to force another to see by our spiritual spectacles (in the form of a book, or some religious or metaphysical way of presenting Truth) and it is not *his* way, it often results in distortion.

Naturally, if there is indication of a need for help, we must stand ready to give it, without forcing our spiritual spectacles upon another person.

We must never confuse the means with the end in our search for Truth. The means will be every outer help that comes our way, but the end is to consciously know (not merely know about) the presence of God within our own soul, which in turn reveals to us our true nature and reason for being.

The Result of an Irritation

HAVE YOU ever looked at a string of pearls, a pearl pin or ring, and thought, "Such beauty!" without realizing what produced the pearls?

On my eighteenth birthday my parents gave me a very lovely string of beads that were covered with mother-of-pearl. To me they were *real* pearls! Then came the day when the string broke while I was away from home. I collected the beads, tied them in a handkerchief, and on my return home put the tied bundle in a drawer. I intended to have the beads restrung, but promptly forgot all about them.

Two years later, I came across this tied handkerchief, not realizing what it contained. When I untied it and saw the pearl beads, thoughts of my father, who had passed away in the mean-time, came to me. I remembered the joy and pride I experienced when I received this birthday gift. As I held the beads in my hand I remember saying to myself: "What about a *real* pearl? How did it come to be formed in the oyster?"

I went to the dictionary, which described a pearl as "a smooth, hard, usually white or bluish gray, abnormal growth . . . formed around a foreign body within the shell of some oysters and certain other mollusks." This intrigued me and I did a bit of further research in an encyclopedia. What it yielded was truly enlightening: "A pearl is formed when some irritating particle causes the oyster to cover it with a protective excretion which in time hardens. The pearl oysters differ from the edible oysters chiefly by the thick mother-of-pearl in the shell." This latter remark was interesting to me because my beads, while not pearls, were covered by mother-of-pearl.

Thinking over what I had read, I reasoned that just because the oyster belongs to a certain species of creation it could not of itself have created the "protective excretion" that we call the pearly substance, nor did the intelligence to do something about the "foreign body" come from the oyster. Lastly, the oyster had not of itself produced the power to apply the substance to encase the irritating particle.

How well I remember that day sitting on my bedroom floor looking at a few beads in my hand with these thoughts running through my mind! They led me to see a correlation between the action of the oyster to eliminate inharmony and the efforts *we* make to get rid of unpleasant situations. I could not help but wonder which of the two species of creation was making a better job of it!

There is much that comes into our human experience that seems so foreign to what we feel we ought to be experiencing. Sometimes there are not only irritating situations regarding our bodies and our financial affairs, but there are unpleasant circumstances in our human relations. Many of these have resulted from misunderstanding, criticism, bias, quarrels, envy, jealousy.

What is the instinctive desire of the oyster when the foreign body causes irritation in its organism? To get rid of the discomfort! The oyster does not go here and there, trying to find a solution. Apparently its instinct is to turn to the indwelling intelligence peculiar to its own species, which prompts it to cover the offending obstacle to its comfort with a substance so smooth that the foreign matter is no longer irritating.

Inbuilt in the oyster is the solution to its problem: the ability to transform an unpleasant condition into one that makes for comfort.

What about the irritating, confusing, unhappy situations that cause me discomfort? As I, too, belong to a species of creation—the human race—surely there is inbuilt in me an intelligence that can meet my particular problem! Unlike the oyster, I have a choice. I can ignore the intelligence within me. I can complain about the circumstances or individuals involved; I can run to others asking advice about what to do. Or perhaps my choice is just to remain in the unpleasant situation, doing nothing to alleviate it. I can say in effect: "Oh, well, that is life. What can you expect?"

If I have a consciousness of who and what I am in God's sight, I can turn to my own indwelling intelligence, which is the God presence ready to serve me when called upon. Following the example of the oyster that does something positive about its undesirable problem, I can let intelligence guide me to transform an irritating situation into "a thing of beauty."

We do not create the substance that can bring about the transformation; this is a creation of God. What is this substance? It is thought-substance that can be molded through love, faith, understanding, and any needed quality to enfold the unhappy problem. Nor do we create the power and intelligence that enable us to bring about the change. God Himself is the author of these, not the human being.

Thoughts such as these went through my mind that day as I let a broken string of pearl beads teach me a spiritual lesson! I was convinced then, as I am now, that it is only God-intelligence, God-power, and God-substance that can enable me to make changes in my life in order that unpleasant, irritating, and confusing experiences may become as a string of pearls. Pearls give a shimmering beauty that cannot fail to lift the heart of one who is conscious of beauty. But the basis for the lovely pearl was certainly not a thing of beauty to the oyster. The little mollusk just got busy improving its own environment, probably not the least concerned whether the result was a vision of beauty, but concerned only with the restoration of comfort.

Apparently the oyster never bothered to look around and blame some other oyster, or the oyster bed, or some outside circumstance. It merely went about its work of producing comfort instead of discomfort, ease instead of irritation, and harmony instead of inharmony. This work was done by using the three ingredients found within itself—intelligence, power, substance— placed there by the Creator.

Are we making "a string of pearls," "a thing of beauty" out of the unfolding events of our life? Most of us respond to beauty in all its various forms, in music, in art, in nature, in our homes—in fact, in all facets of our living. Unpleasant and uncomfortable things take our minds away from that which is our natural inclination, and we therefore seek a solution to the problems that are upsetting.

If we have an understanding of Truth, we can bring beauty, comfort, and harmony in place of that which is causing us distress. We only add to the distress by bemoaning, blaming, criticizing. Once convinced that we *can* do something, we turn through prayer to the God-intelligence within that handles the know-how for every species of creation. In us, it goes far beyond the instinct of the animal kingdom into spiritual understanding, available to us in all areas and at all periods of our life.

When the indwelling intelligence moves in us we think of it as guidance. Guidance from whom? From the God presence within us.

Scripture states: "You will decide on a matter, and it will be established for you, and light will shine on your ways." Our first step should be to decree or affirm that the good we seek is already ours in Truth, in Spirit. On the surface it may seem that we are stating something that has nothing to do with the matter at hand. Closer observation indicates that we are molding in thought-substance the kind of experience we want. By our decree we are establishing a pattern for thought-substance to follow in reshaping the negative into the positive, just as the oyster reshapes the disturbing particle into a thing of beauty.

We need power to erase from our mind all the negative pictures we have been holding and to affirm the good we want to demonstrate; then, above all, patience! Undoubtedly the oyster uses much patience to accomplish its purpose, making smooth that which is rough and harsh. It may require much patience on our part to build new mental pictures regarding our finances, our bodies, our human relations. This patience must be based on the faith that sees beyond the limited human condition.

Perhaps to some it may seem foolish to affirm life, strength, and health in the very face of pain, suffering, or imperfection. Once we understand that by affirmation we are drawing on God's intelligence, power, and substance to build a mental pattern for the body to follow, it no longer seems foolish.

Perhaps finances are at so low an ebb that one feels panicky, afraid, and alone. Our turning consciously in prayer to the indwelling intelligence of God gives us the assurance that God is the one Creator and thus the one Source of all supply. Charles Fillmore says, ''It is perfectly logical to assume that a wise and competent Creator would provide for the needs of His creatures in their various stages of growth.''

Consciously calling on the intelligence of God moves into action the power necessary to mold mind-substance into patterns that can bring forth the outer forms of prosperity.

What about situations involving another individual or individuals? How can we turn an unpleasant, unhappy human relationship into a pearl? If we have "ears to hear" as Jesus said, the indwelling God-intelligence will remind us that each person is a spiritual being. Going a little further, another realization is vital: each of us is an evolving soul. Each is growing at his own pace; each is seeing life from his own vantage point of soul unfoldment. This understanding helps to prevent criticism of self or another and, enfolding the relationship in love, we find that we have made another pearl in life!

What a string of pearls we have already put together! Yes, we can produce pearls. If someone has spoken unkindly or critically, instead of a like retort, we can react in love and understanding—and one more pearl has been produced! We have smoothed over the awkward moment by using the spiritual resources at our disposal. A happy solution, like the pearl in the oyster, has resulted from an irritation that might have caused very strained relations with another person.

Psychologists say that in many cases the critical

or harsh word, the striking out in bitterness, is the cry of a soul for help. If we have any understanding of Truth at all, we will respond to such cries as befits a child of God. In such case, we will produce a pearl of happiness in place of anguish and suffering. The improved relations will indeed be the result of an irritation.

Perhaps each of us needs to ask himself: "Am I making a string of pearls out of the events of my daily living? Or am I allowing rough obstacles to come between enjoyment in life for myself as well as for those close to me and for all whom I will contact?" No one but the individual can answer this question.

It is evidence that Truth has been victorious when even the memory of an unpleasant event has been turned into a pearl.

Each overcoming we make, through the intelligence, power, and mind-substance of God, is transforming some disagreeable occurrence into that which more nearly fits God's plan of good for us. From the overcoming of the irritation has resulted a thing of beauty, which the poet Keats says will be "a joy forever."

Surely the greatest of all pearls is our consciousness of the "pearl of great price," which has resulted from the revelation of truth about God, about ourself, about our fellow human beings, and about the world in which we live. Where previously we may have had a limited and even fearful approach to life, a whole new concept comes when we let God's intelligence unveil the truth that sets us free from limitation of any kind. We are obligated to construct the pearl of Truth in consciousness if we would fulfill our mission in life.

No Trespassing

AT ONE time or another most of us have been faced with this question: "How far can I go in pointing out to a relative, a friend, or even a chance acquaintance a need for change in conduct or actions?"

In a class I recently attended, the chapter "Loose Him and Let Him Go" from H. Emilie Cady's book *How I Used Truth* was under discussion. The primary subject was: Has one person the right to interfere with another's life? A teacher attending the class made this significant remark: "When we interfere with another's life in the sense of telling him what or what not to do, we are trespassing."

The word *trespassing* had quite an impact on

me. It presented a viewpoint I had not previously considered. The word stayed with me, and on reaching home I checked the dictionary. Among the definitions of the word *trespass,* I found some enlightening statements. First of all, the root meaning of trespass is to go across or over. Now give thought to these ideas that I gained from my perusal. Trespass is to exceed the bounds of what is lawful, right, just; to encroach as on another's privileges, rights, privacy; to intrude on what belongs to another; to go outside one's sphere; to violate a right or prerogative. A challenge is presented in each of these ideas.

What about our part regarding those close to us, those with whom we live, work, or have social contacts? To what lengths may we go without trespassing on another's privacy?

In the discussion that ensued in the class referred to, the following was quoted from the chapter under consideration: ''No one has any right to coerce another to accept his ideal. Every person has a right to keep his own ideal until he desires to change it.''

But what are we to do? Stand by and let that one move toward an unpleasant situation? Do we not have a responsibility? Of course we do!

Dr. Cady says, "You can, whenever you think of your friend, speak the word of freedom to him."

We respect a "No Trespassing" sign on a piece of property. Why is it then that there are areas in the lives of persons whose lives touch ours, even superficially, upon which we sometimes feel we have the right to encroach? The obvious answer is that we may feel that our love and concern for another give us the right to try to show him where he is wrong. Yet, do we have the right (unless he is too young to have evaluated right and wrong) to say, "You should not be doing this or that?" Should we not respect the "No Trespassing" sign in his life, invisible though it may be?

Some words attributed to the Greek Stoic philosopher, Epictetus, seem as modern as any to fit the subject of no trespassing in the lives of others: "Does any one bathe hastily? Do not say that he does it ill, but hastily. Does any one drink much wine? Do not say that he does ill, but that he drinks a great deal. For unless you perfectly understand his motives, how should you know if he acts ill? Thus you will not risk yielding to any appearances but such as you fully comprehend."

It is not only when we consider that another is doing something wrong that we are often guilty of trespassing, but when we make remarks (often unconsciously) in a critical attitude. "Why are you wearing your hair that way?" "Why don't you change that piece of furniture to another place?" "Don't eat that particular food, it's bad for you." All of these remarks, while quite correct from *our* viewpoint, are actually trespassing, for they encroach on another's privileges, rights, and privacy. We are exceeding the bounds of what is right in human relationships. Instead of helping, our attitude may cause the other person to bristle and close himself to that which might add more satisfaction to his life.

In the area of soul unfoldment, any attempt to trespass can be very touchy. Perhaps we have found something that has changed our life and we want to share it; we want a loved one to know the joy which we have experienced. Our desire to share may exceed what is right. We may be guilty of proselyting, which is an attempt to change another's way of thinking and acting to one that fits our standard.

On the other hand, a gentle, loving suggestion, often posed as a question, can help another reach a broader approach in his thinking and acting; we shall not have been guilty of trespassing on his right to make his own choices.

There are times, however, when even a suggestion is better left unsaid. In cases where a suggestion seems warranted, it can be made in such a way that the other person recognizes that there is no intent to intrude on his privacy, thus hostility does not enter into the picture.

We have no right—certainly God did not give it to us—to infringe on another's right to find God in his own way. To be ready to give assistance when asked directly or indirectly is quite a different matter. Sometimes the request for help is not in actual words but one can sense the unconscious reaching out for it. If we keep close to our own inner spiritual center, God will guide us as to what help we need to render.

There are two ways of looking at the biblical question ''Am I my brother's keeper?'' I am *not* my brother's keeper in the sense that I keep my eyes on his actions, seeking to prod him to make changes when his conduct does not fit my standards. I *am* my brother's keeper in the sense that I continue to keep in mind that he is a child of

God, as I am, seeking in his own way to unfold his divine nature.

It is quite true that while a child is in his growing years, the parent or guardian must give outer guidance. The parent or guardian can help the child only at his own level of unfoldment. Once, however, the child reaches what is popularly termed the age of discretion, the parent or guardian must learn to ''loose him and let him go.'' Yes, even to making his own mistakes, as difficult as this may be.

God has created us with inner abilities to handle our own life. Each seed has within itself the pattern of life, enabling it to bring forth after its kind. We, too, have a pattern of life placed in us at our creation—the image and likeness of God. Just as with the seed, our divine pattern enables us to bring forth that which is right for us at any given time.

The seed must have right growing conditions in order to produce according to its species. We, too, must have right conditions in our minds, any coercing of free choice prevents the production of good in our life. It is no wonder that Jesus presented the two love commandments—first to love God and then one's neighbor—for love never imposes upon the privileges, rights, or privacy of our neighbor.

I once heard that no leaf on a plant or tree completely obscures another leaf, so that each has access to light. Each plant must utilize the nutrients of soil, air, water, as needed and in its own way. How foolish for the tropical plant, needing a lot of moisture, to say to the desert cactus, "Oh, you need more water!" Some of us, having both types of plants in our home or garden, have found to our sorrow the unhappy result of treating both types of plants the same insofar as watering is concerned.

Of course, we may feel that our loved one, friend, or neighbor would be happier, healthier, more successful had he more awareness of Truth. But it is not our business to tell him so.

On a journey overseas, my mother agreed to include in her itinerary a trip to Scotland to visit the sister of a friend of mine. Nothing was said during my mother's visit about religion, but after her return to our home in Canada, the woman in Scotland wrote in a letter to me, "What is it that your mother has that makes her so happy, confident, and a joy to be around?" This was just the opening I needed! In my reply I told her about Unity and had literature sent to her. Needless to say, she became an enthusiastic Truth student. My mother was herself a sermon on Truth rather than merely voicing it, which might have constituted a trespassing on this woman's particular religious path.

After suggesting that we speak the word of freedom to him when we are concerned over the actions of another person, H. Emilie Cady says, "You can tell him mentally that Christ lives within him, and makes him free." She then warns us not to recognize any manifestation other than the good in him. This may seem a tall order for us. It really means that we refuse to acknowledge some error or backsliding as having reality; it cannot have reality, because God did not create it. We are actually following the injunction of Jesus, "Do not judge by appearances, but judge with right judgment."

Do you recall that as a child if someone said to you, "Don't do that!" it was the one thing above all that you wanted to do right then! If a child or adult feels that he is being imposed upon, the desire to lash out is inevitable. Perhaps the founding fathers of the United

States of America discerned this in referring to man's inalienable rights.

If a person acts against the laws of society, he brings about his own punishment; it is not some governing or policing body that trespasses on his rights, but rather he himself who trespasses on the rights of others and brings his own unhappy results. His freedom as an individual does not give him license to do that which is contrary to the laws of life.

A vital point to consider is this: the endeavor to abide by the no trespassing policy must not produce an attitude of indifference. If anything, our desire to leave others free keeps us open and receptive to God's guidance for any move on our part to help in a human relationship. We will know what we need to do—if anything—in the outer without our trespassing on another's life style. Often it may be no more than, as Dr. Cady suggests, speaking the word and knowing the truth about that one. We can see the importance of prayer in keeping our mind clear of negation, of criticism; the importance of our prayer for another to help him handle his life in ways that lead to fulfillment.

All Night Coming

Morning has been all night coming.
But see how certainly it comes.
—James Dillet Freeman

MORNING has been all night coming. We could take this to mean that the answer to some need or problem has had a gulf of darkness to bridge. To the one involved in this period of darkness, there may seem to be no way out of some distressing situation. The hours of waiting seem endless. But morning *will come,* even though it has been "all night coming."

Charles Fillmore interprets *day* as being "the state of mind in which intelligence dominates." He refers on the other hand to *night* as "the realm of thoughts that are not yet illuminated by the Spirit of God." *Morning* represents the dawning of light in our mind, the illumination or realization of the answer to a problem that may have been plaguing us so long. *Night* can be interpreted as a period when there seems to be a stalemate regarding the outcome of some experience or problem.

An Eastern philosopher and poet, Rabindranath Tagore, has said, "Faith is the bird that feels the light and sings when the dawn is still dark!" When we can have faith, though all is yet dark, then our soul has the conviction that morning certainly will come. In the Bible we read:

For still the vision awaits its time;
*   it hastens to the end—it will not lie.*
If it seem slow, wait for it;
*   it will surely come, it will not delay.*

Most of us, seeking answers to our problems, have at least a vague vision of the good we wish to see manifested. When we consider the words "If it seem slow, wait for it," can we not take this to refer to having patience? Keeping faith in our vision often requires an almost super faith made possible through the patience that can wait calmly in spite of appearances.

Meeting undesirable situations at the outset is often not too difficult, but when the resolving of the problem seems delayed, it is then that our patience is strained to the utmost. Doubts creep in, fear and anxiety take over, until there seems to be an impregnable wall of darkness surrounding us. The man with a family to provide for who is suddenly laid off work knows his own financial situation. His imagination sees, in the face of rising costs in the world, his resources being depleted so that he cannot meet his standard of living. He may try to keep his fears and anxieties from his family but they come out in many ways, until tension arises in the home. He may blame himself for the situation, or blame others or circumstances. This attitude of blame does not help but adds to the darkness or night which seems to be swamping his whole thinking processes.

This man needs something to hold on to. This is where he can call on the by-product of faith that we call patience. He may be tempted to feel that with the closing of one channel for his income, there is no evidence of another door opening. But patience will keep him steady in mind and action so that he will take whatever steps are necessary. It requires patience to know that the morning will come; to know that though his vision of the new job or avenue of service seems slow in manifesting, it will surely come. The patience he exercises in this situation will build a consciousness of expectancy and enthusiasm, and not only will he bring to his new place of service his own unique skills and talents but a new attitude, a new approach to life.

Patience keeps us true to our vision of good; it prevents our mind from getting confused and despondent. Patience enables us to handle the various situations that arise in human relationships, because it is based on the faith that sees beyond the outer happenings.

Through years of teaching I have had conversations with and letters from persons who have felt a hopelessness concerning some human relationship. I have been struck by the anguish so often revealed. It would seem that there must be love somewhere in the whole situation; otherwise, why the anguish? The wife sorrowing over an alcoholic husband; a husband in despair over a wife's attitude of jealousy, indifference, or unreasonable demands; the son or daughter desperately seeking to be free from domination of mother or father, stemming undoubtedly from the parental love that fears losing the child. All of these situations weigh heavy on the heart and it takes great patience to hold fast to a faith that perceives a good outcome.

In business we see the employer who feels that his workers are deliberately crossing him right and left, having little loyalty to him or to his business. On the other end are the employees, who feel they are being exploited by the employer. It is not an easy task for these individuals to have patience to know that good results can come forth without a complete breakdown of relations.

Individuals make up nations, so what works in the individual life can also work in relations between the peoples of the world. Patience requires that prejudices and preconceived opinions be laid aside and the whole attention placed on what we desire to see made manifest and not on what we fear may occur.

How hemmed in, how bound we feel when sickness or disease attacks the physical body. In this darkness of pain and suffering—and perhaps in something that is causing us even more anguish, the fear about the outcome—it is not easy to believe that the dawn will come. We need the deep assurance that can come only from a faith that is strengthened by the type of understanding that says: "There is a right outcome. Have patience. See how certainly it comes!" Peace takes over in our consciousness and patience—patience that is no longer a kind of resignation, but a deep knowing that all is well.

Whether for our own healing or that of another, the inner assurance that comes turns the darkness into morning, even though the latter has been "all night coming." So far as human time is concerned there might still be days or weeks until the outer manifestation comes, but the inner morning that has dawned makes a solid foundation upon which to stand.

We have heard the statement that the answer is contained within the question; certainly the morning of enlightenment is contained within the night of seeming darkness—the situation that seems impossible of solution, whether it be one of illness, inharmony, lack, confusion, or despair.

Most of us are well aware of the things we are facing, but sometimes how we long for someone to say: "Just hang on. Know the Truth. Know the right answer will come." We need someone to say: "You can do it! You can hold fast to the vision that God wants only good for you (or your loved one)."

It is quite possible for any of us to be so convinced of the good outcome of some situation that we actually become impatient at not seeing the outer change. We may feel that there is delay or failure if our physical eyes cannot observe the answer we seek. It is one thing to say, "There is no time in Spirit," yet we need also to realize that there is an orderly unfoldment of the expressions of life on the outer plane of existence. Much patience, much knowing the Truth becomes a part of the orderly unfoldment of God's plan in our life. Yes, though the night of uncertainty, doubt, fear, and limitation seems to hide the morning or the vision, certainly it will surely come.

What problem in your life, or that of a dear one, has need of your understanding patience? True patience must be based upon the faith that perceives good as our inheritance. It would almost seem that our very desire to change unpleasant happenings must in itself be a proof that at least subconsciously we feel that good is ours by right of existence.

Learning to have patience is not an easy task. Consider the inventor to whom the full-blown idea seems so real. Surely he must have moments of frustration when impatience enters in. He must wonder why the outer product does not conform immediately to the idea or plan he holds in his mind. Yet the true genius knows that all life is an unfolding; he does not look at his experiments as failures, as the world may view them, but rather as stepping-stones to the ultimate success.

The dressmaker or tailor who would throw up a project because something did not seem to fit, would not be considered very reliable. Rather, he would look again to the pattern, do whatever is necessary to correct the error, then proceed. This must of necessity take patience.

We look and listen to the accomplished musician, observing his smooth performance. What we do not know, though we may surmise, are the hours of frustration he must have had, the impatience he must have experienced before he was able to present the composition in its best production.

If you and I know that something needs changing in our life, if we feel that we are entitled to something better than we are presently manifesting, if the morning we seek with its resultant good has been ''all night coming,'' can we not apply the attitude of patience and so build our consciousness into a firm faith that accepts the good outcome? This does not mean that we ignore the experiences in the outer, for so often they are warnings that we have gotten off the track. However, we no longer allow them to influence us to believe that there will not be the good outcome we desire. It is possible to view the outer circumstance, which seems at the moment to indicate failure, as an indication that progress is being made in spite of the appearance. What may seem to you to be a failure to demonstrate health, prosperity, or harmony may only be a period when you are strengthening your mental and spiritual muscles so that you are able to meet the responsibilities that will come with the changed circumstances in your life.

Yes, morning may have been all night coming, but standing firmly on the Truth can assure you how certainly it comes. Look back into your life. Have there not been times when you thought there was something you wanted, either in circumstances or in things, that you did not get? Yet, there came a time when something much more satisfactory came into your life. Perhaps there had been impatience when you did not get what you thought you wanted, but there was something higher than your human wanting that somehow prevented you from getting the lesser so that when you were ready the greater good could come into your life's expression.

It is easy for anyone to give in to impatience, and it often makes us say things we regret. It is the mark of the true overcomer to know that while ''morning has been all night coming'' we can with a steady mind ''see how certainly it comes.''

Destiny at My Command

HAVE you ever wondered how many people in the world are really convinced that mankind has a destiny of good?

From the beginning of my Truth study I was willing to accept, at first intellectually, the idea that each one of us has a destiny of good toward which he is moving at his own soul's pace. Yet the full force of this realization never became so clear as during a Unity service a few months ago. For years I had heard and sung the metaphysical words written to the tune of the dear and familiar hymn "Rock of Ages." Now, as we sang the words, "On the rock of Truth I stand, /Destiny at my command" something seemed to light up inside of me! These words, *destiny at my com-*

mand, took on a new meaning. Right then and there my mind began to question: "What is my destiny? How is it at my command?"

One of my great joys is sharing and discussing Truth ideas with those of like mind. During a conversation with Ernest C. Wilson, I mentioned my interest in the idea of destiny at my command. He startled and challenged me with the remark, "But your destiny is already established."

"Don't I have anything to do with my destiny?" I asked.

"Oh, yes," Dr. Wilson said. "It is what you do about your destiny that is of importance to you. Let me illustrate: If you wish to go to New York City, that is your destination, or if you will, your destiny. The way you get there is, however, 'at your command.' But if you do not get there, New York City will still be there! Remember it is only what you do about attaining your destiny that is at your command."

Of course, Dr. Wilson is quite correct. Nothing can change God's plan or destiny for us. God has destined us to be in manifestation what He has decreed for us—to be His image-likeness. This means to experience good, God's good, in mind, body, and affairs.

How is this done? If God's plan (destiny) for us is in the abstract, how do we make it concrete? A scriptural verse comes to mind as being apropos: "You will decide on a matter, and it will be established for you, and light will shine on your ways." And in the New Testament we have the remark of the centurion to Jesus concerning his servant's need for healing: "Say the word, and let my servant be healed." Decree. Say the word. In other words, "Affirm the Truth."

In Truth as presented by Unity, this "decreeing," "saying," or "speaking" comes under the heading of affirmation.

What occurs when a strong affirmation of Truth is uttered silently or audibly? A definite change of a positive nature takes place in the mind, the consciousness. The idea back of the words draws thought substance to the idea and builds what Emmet Fox calls a "mental equivalent." As the idea back of the word has drawn the invisible mind substance to form a mental picture, so this mental equivalent acts as a magnet to draw manifest substance to clothe the idea in some tangible form—a home, clothes, food, a job, a trip, harmonious human relationships, happiness, success.

In order that our divine destiny may manifest in practical ways, the mind must be clear and calm so that the thinking and feeling processes may handle the events and circumstances of everyday living in the best possible way. Decreeing, speaking the word, with a clear, calm mind is a step in taking command of our destiny, a step toward claiming that which is ours by divine right. If there is a need of bodily healing, we decree the word of life, vitality, strength, in the full knowledge that life is our birthright, that to be healthy is our destiny. Should there be lack in our finances, we decree that God is the one source of all good. By our spoken word we take command of our thinking. Rather than thinking in terms of lack, we decree the infilling of God's substance. To be prosperous and successful is our destiny.

Probably mankind suffers as much, if not more, from unhappy human relations than from lack of health or money. Yet, having accepted the truth that happiness, satisfaction, and fulfillment are part of our divine destiny, we find that we can take command of our thinking and feeling so that unhappy situations can be resolved. Here again our affirming Truth—our speaking the word of happiness, satisfaction, and fulfillment—helps to call forth the harmony and peace we desire.

There is no magic in merely speaking positive words. What is the real value of decrees or affirmations? In the first few months of my Truth study, I could not bring myself to speak what Unity termed affirmations of Truth, because I could not see that they were truthful. It seemed foolish to make certain decrees about health when I was aware of ill-health and pain. Or to speak of abundance as being mine when I knew there was lack in my finances. Or to state that harmony and love were abounding when I was keenly aware of inharmony and unhappiness. However, as the months went by, my exposure to Truth teachings brought me to the place where I could affirm statements of Truth. I was not sure why they worked, though I personally saw their efficacy in my own life within a period of a few months.

It was these words in the writings of Charles Fillmore that brought me a step higher in understanding. In discussing affirmations of Truth, he says: "These affirmations often are so far beyond the present attainment of the novice as to seem ridiculous, but when it is understood that the statements are grouped about an ideal to be attained, they seem fair and reasonable."

The words, *grouped about an ideal to be attained,* made clear to me the whole reason for affirmations. If we are suffering ill-health, then it is logical to assume that what we want to attain is vital health, strength, and wholeness, so we present this ideal to our consciousness. If we feel that we have need of tangible substance in the form of money, things, a job, a home, then it does seem fair and reasonable that we direct our mind to the positive attitudes that will allow life to manifest what is needed. No one wishing to succeed would study about failure: his ideal is success, and he directs all of his energies toward that end.

By affirming, speaking the word, decreeing some good, we are directing our mental energies toward the manifestation of our destiny in mind, body, and affairs.

The choice belongs to each of us. Shall we decree that which is true of us as spiritual beings? Or shall we allow the mind to harbor the fears, anxieties, and limitations that keep us from attaining our divine destiny?

If we feel discouraged over a problem, it is astonishing how we can talk ourselves out of it simply by affirming that which is true of God and thus true of us whom He created in His own image and after His likeness.

If a person were to receive a communication from a law firm that he had been given a bequest under a will, he would not leave the matter there. It would be up to him to take action to substantiate his claim before he could receive the tangible bequest. Certainly it would be his according to law, but his part would be to make his claim and press his claim.

To affirm is to claim in mind. To persist in affirming good where none seems apparent is to press one's claim.

The practice of affirming Truth is rather like the five-finger exercises the pianist finds necessary before he can become the finely tuned channel through which the beauty of music may find free expression. These exercises, practiced over and over, make it possible for the mind, like the fingers of the musician, to claim the harmonies that are to be brought forth.

When faced with a condition of sickness, does it seem to you to be inadequate just to affirm that God's life is yours by divine right and flows through the cells of your body? Does it seem a little foolish at first to make statements about abundance when your pocketbook and bank account are empty? Does it seem ridiculous to affirm that harmony, understanding, and love are at work in some human situation which is making you sick at heart? These are natural human reactions. But in Truth we seek to go beyond the human acceptance to the divine assurance.

Once you make a definite habit of decreeing, of speaking the word, of affirming the Truth, you will find that it is neither inadequate, foolish, nor ridiculous. You will get results that will attest to the efficacy of the process. It is then that you will become aware of inner mastery and finally reach the inner conviction that destiny is at your command.

While our true destiny as a child of God is already established, it lies within our power to make this destiny tangible in our everyday living. We may read and study and seek to do good works, but until we speak the word that will release us from mental bondage and affirm the truth about our self and our world, we will not experience the good in mind, body, and affairs to which our destiny entitles us. We cannot stand idly by, even with a knowledge of Truth, and expect our good to become tangible in our life. We are the ones who must make the conscious necessary effort. To repeat, we must claim our good and press our claim. It may be necessary for us to affirm over and over the Truth concerning some situation. At another time, it may be that just to speak the word brings instant results, as it did in the case of the healing of the centurion's servant.

Much will depend on how ready our mind is to accept our destiny of good. This good takes many forms, and it will vary with each person and with each point in time. For some it will be the right home, loving companions; for others a career or profession that is satisfying and fulfilling. Vibrant health of body may be the most urgent need for others; success and abundance may be the sought-after goal of others. Peace of mind, assurance of God's care for a loved one, may be the predominant desire of other hearts.

If you would manifest your destiny, you must,

in the words of James Dillet Freeman: "Dare to believe that God is your health; dare to believe that He is your support; dare to believe that you have in you all the ideas that you will ever need for a happy and successful life; dare to be generous, loving, free."

Only dreams? No! Dreams become actualities as you take the step of recognizing your own divine destiny, your own inheritance, and follow that with the action of decreeing, of speaking the word, of affirming Truth.

Destiny *is* at your command!

About My Father's Business:
No Circumstance
Can Separate Me from My Good

I HAVE OFTEN said, perhaps more glibly than consciously, "No circumstance can separate me from my good." I learned this in my early days of study from the book, *Lessons in Truth.* In it, H. Emilie Cady says, "No person or thing in the universe, no chain of circumstances, can by any possibility interpose itself between you and all joy—all good."

After months of sickness, I challenged this statement, when everything in the outer seemed to belie it. With all my heart I knew I believed that nothing could separate me from my good, yet appearances denied it. Then suddenly a revelation seemed to flash into my consciousness. I saw that when I said, "my good," I was likely to be thinking of some ultimate good to be attained. Now I realized that my good takes many forms and comes in varying degrees. For instance, during the enforced inactivity I was experiencing, there were periods when I felt that my good was a few minutes relief from pain, or cool, fresh air after the stifling heat of an extremely hot day or night. Then I grasped the truth that to recognize and acknowledge any form of good, no matter how small, was to be "about my Father's business."

Think of a boy or girl at, say, age twelve, stating emphatically, "I am going to be a medical doctor." Here is the first intimation of an ultimate good to be mentally and physically attained. But what a lot has to be done in that young life between age twelve and adulthood. There are the natural periods of growing up, the schooling, recreation, learning to be a part of society, and then the specialized training that will lead to the doctor's degree.

But, and this I can see is important, does not every stage of life from age twelve to the final graduation as a medical doctor make up the final and ultimate goal—the little things, the disciplining of the mind, all that is entailed in working toward the goal of being a doctor? So each event offers its challenges but also its portion of good.

The one who has physical challenges to meet may think that circumstances have separated him from his good or ultimate healing, but if he sees each improvement as good, then he can say in all sincerity, "No circumstance can separate me from my good," meaning the good of daily living as well as the ultimate attainment of health. Thus he is about his Father's business, the business of seeing good.

Can one who has suffered bereavement, perhaps the death of a life partner, say this statement? Yes, because no one, no circumstance can take away the good already experienced. And the relationship can only enrich the unfolding good as the bereaved one adjusts to changing circumstances, learns to overcome loneliness, seeks to rely on inner resources, adds to others' enjoyment of life by indicating that the now-physically-severed relationship enriched his life rather than left it embittered.

What about finances? When everything seems at a standstill and circumstances (loss of job, preponderance of debts, desertion or death of the

one who had represented financial support) seem
a barrier to good, can one truly say, "No circumstance can separate me from my good"? Yes!
Why? Because we cannot be separated from
God, the one source of good. In fact, such circumstances can, properly viewed, call forth
abilities of which one was seemingly unaware,
allowing an even greater inflow of material
substance to come into the individual's life.

Covering these general categories of circumstances that many of us meet along life's
pathway, the thing we must learn to face is that
when we say "our good" it may seem to be an
ultimate state or condition, but in reality it is
made up of many degrees and forms of good.

During a particularly hot Missouri summer, I
was bedridden. While my longing was for a
quick healing, the urgent need of the moment
was for coolness. An air conditioner was ordered
by telephone (after five years in our apartment
with no need for one!). We were told that it
might be days before it could be installed. The
Daily Word statement and meditation for that
day dealt with *decisions*. Our order for the air
conditioner was put in; a decision had been
made. The next step was up to God.

Early the next morning a call from a delivery firm came to advise that the air conditioner would be installed within two hours! The young man doing the work said that what they did not get installed that day would have to wait four days! The point is this: having made a decision, we left an open channel for God to work through. This was certainly for good. So no circumstance had separated us from the desired good in the form of air conditioning.

It is possible, even after having made a decision, to interfere with the smooth outworking of a decision by doubts, fears, and anxieties. Because the *Daily Word* message for that day had been on decisions, I was able to push aside all the "But suppose we can't get an air conditioner when we need it" type of thoughts and leave the carrying out to God.

Looking for signs of good, little glimmers of light, faint though they be, is preparing the consciousness for the ultimate good or goal, for the outworking in divine order.

Can one in pain be encouraged by a short period without pain, or by finding a little more strength than had been experienced? Yes. The more learned today may scoff at the formula offered by Dr. Coué, "Every day in every way I'm getting better and better." However, is this not the attitude most medical practitioners would prefer to see? Is it not related to the "imagery" being advanced by holistic medicine today?

If we cannot see the slight improvements in healing, finances, human relationships, how are we to move forward to be ready for the ultimate good we seek?

The one who faces life with an alcoholic husband or wife, or a loved one under the influence of drugs, or any of the demeaning habits that drag men and women down, must, if he or she would be victorious, acknowledge the slight improvements. These are like wedges in the closed door. More than ever, therefore, the full dependence must be on God in order that the faint upward action is allowed to continue. Too often one is apt to say, "I knew it wouldn't last," referring to a slight improvement in any of the circumstances referred to.

If one were in a tunnel following a small light, it would be instinctive to keep the attention and vision on the small light, never wavering but going forward confidently. Why can we not feel as confident with the small improvement we observe?

It takes faith, of course, to keep steadfast. Faith, however, is not based on what one sees in the outer but on inner knowingness. Would you not say that faith coupled with imagination produces what an early writer (Henry Victor Morgan) referred to as the "chamber of imagery"? Faith perceives the good and imagination pictures or conceives it. Thus a pattern is set up for the mind (thinking and feeling) to follow. This is assuming that what has been pictured in the "chamber of imagery" is good. Human beings have the right of choice in the use of their mind. If what is pictured is good, then good must result in the outer world. Conversely, if negative pictures have been allowed to form the pattern of thinking and feeling, then by the undeviating law of mind action, the results will be undesirable.

Our good cannot be taken from us, but we must claim it. Consider this illustration: An individual has a savings account at a bank. If he should be in difficulty, the bank manager or any other bank officer cannot say, "So and so is in need, let us give him some of the money in his account." No! He has to make the claim himself.

No matter how great our outer needs—health, finances, harmony in human relations—even God Himself must wait for our claim on the universal good that is there for us. We claim it by our thinking and feeling, following the mind patterns formed by faith, imagination, in fact, all of the divine qualities.

Each little seed in the dark earth calls on its own inner resources so that it may draw all the outer sustenance needed for growth. So with us.

To be able to recognize each step in growth into the greater manifestation is part of being about our Father's business. We learn to recognize our place in the scheme of things and seek to live to the highest we are aware of at each level of unfoldment.

To know (not merely to know about) our spiritual relationship to God is the first step of being about the Father's business. But a close second step must be to see every bit of revealed good, even if small, as part of the greater good. When we see God's presence in the smallest evidence of good, then our lives must change for the better.

One more point concerning our good is the

part others play in our acceptance and claiming of it.

> *More things are wrought by prayer*
> *Than this world dreams of.*
> > *Wherefore, let thy voice*
> *Rise like a fountain for me night and*
> > *day.*

The prayers of others help to keep us true to the goal we seek. The prayers of others help to lift our minds and hearts so that we are much more prepared to accept our good, even the small forms of it.

The astonishing results of personal prayers and the prayers of others in our behalf are certainly beyond our greatest expectations. Just as we seem about to give up, to feel that we cannot attain our good, an unexpected renewal of spirit comes to us and we feel: "I must keep on. I must believe." Very often this is because of the loving prayers of those who care. These prayers help us erase the negative pictures in our "chamber of imagery."

Pray for yourself. Pray that the good that is yours by divine right may manifest in your outer life, even if only in small degrees at first. But pray for others even as they pray for you, for by the very act of prayer, "more things are wrought . . . than this world dreams of." The lifting of the mind and heart in prayer not only brings our good, against which no negative circumstance can prevail, but it adds to the uplift of the world.

Printed U.S.A.   150-F-4659-20M-2-81